Christianity and Democracy are so intimately interwoven that every man who has seized power for the destruction of Democracy has first discarded his religion and then waged a war on Christianity and on God Himself. Democracy is based on the rights and dignity of the individual and a smooth running Democracy must depend on the right thinking and the right acting of individuals. Christianity has the same basis, and its aim is to promote right thinking and right living.

Democracy is based on the truth that "all men are created equal," and so is Christianity.

Democracy assumes that men are possessed of inalienable rights, flowing directly from the Creator, and so does Christianity. Christianity and even the Creator Himself must be gotten out of the way before a dictator can successfully complete his program. This is the verdict both of history and of Christian philosophy and theology.

Under the sort of Democracy which was contemplated by Thomas Jefferson, who wrote our Declaration of Independence, there should never be a conflict between the Government of the United States and the Catholic Church, because the philosophy of the Declaration of Independence is the philosophy of the Church.

— MOST REV. JOHN F. NOLL
IN HIS BOOK *THE DECLINE OF NATIONS*

PATRIOTIC
LEADERS
of the CHURCH

PATRIOTIC LEADERS of the CHURCH

JOHN F. FINK

Our Sunday Visitor Publishing Division

Our Sunday Visitor, Inc.

Huntington, Indiana 46750

Copyright © 2004 by Our Sunday Visitor Publishing Division, Our Sunday Visitor, Inc. Published 2004
09 08 07 06 05 04   1 2 3 4 5

Our Sunday Visitor Publishing Division
Our Sunday Visitor, Inc.
200 Noll Plaza
Huntington, IN 46750

ISBN: 1-59276-074-0 (Inventory No. T125)
LCCN: 2004108872

Cover design by Troy Lefevra
Interior design by Sherri L. Hoffman
Interior art by Margaret Bunson

PRINTED IN THE UNITED STATES OF AMERICA

CONTENTS

FOREWORD

There has been an upsurge in patriotism among Americans since the terrorist attacks on our country on September 11, 2001. Our flag is displayed more frequently, we hear "America the Beautiful" and other patriotic songs sung more often, and the United States seems to be more united than it was before that tragic day.

No group of people has been participating more in that patriotism — that demonstration of love for our country — than have Catholics. For one thing, a disproportionately high number of Catholics were killed when the terrorists attacked, especially among New York City's police and firemen. More than that, though, it seems to be part of the nature of American Catholics to display their affection for their country. It has happened over and over throughout the history of the United States.

It seems, however, that American Catholics often are not aware of the patriotism which many of the leaders of their Church have displayed throughout history. It can be no accident that the greatest leaders of the Catholic Church in America have also been among its greatest patriots. That is the rationale and the thesis of this book.

These men were from periods of history considerably different from America at the beginning of the twenty-first century. For most of our country's history, anti-Catholicism was widespread. If there is considerably less anti-Catholicism in America today, much of the credit should go to men such as those profiled in this book. Their stories cannot be told without some emphasis on their efforts to combat the anti-Catholicism of their days.

The reader may wonder why there needs to be any emphasis on the patriotism of Catholic leaders. Who is questioning it? Well, there were plenty of people who were questioning it during previous periods of our history. While it is pleasing that there is today less of a tendency to question Catholics' civic loyalty, we cannot fully appreciate the strides Catholics have made in our society without understanding the struggles many went through to achieve this.

Catholics should be more knowledgeable about the patriotism of the priests and prelates who are a part of our American history. These men chosen to tell this story are all official, ordained representatives of one religious and cultural tradition. They are leaders of the Catholic Church who lived during periods when our national life was meeting various crises and undergoing significant changes — intellectual, social, political, and economic. They played prominent and decisive roles in both the religious and civil life of their day.

We must face another question: How appropriate is it, in this ecumenical age, to review some of the unpleasant facts of Catholic-Protestant controversy? I can only reply that the stories of these men could not be told honestly without reference to such conflicts. They lived when it was common to take strong positions on religious issues and to debate them sharply and vigorously. They encountered organized forces of anti-Catholic bigotry and felt themselves obliged to deal with them in defense of truth. They were both strong defenders of the Catholic Faith and among the greatest patriots the United States has ever known. We all will benefit by becoming.

Naturally, the stories presented here are hardly complete portraits of these men. In the limited scope of this book, they are profiles. They have all been the subjects of much larger books. I hope, though, that I've presented enough information about them for the reader to appreciate the importance of these men in the history of both our Church and our country.

ACKNOWLEDGEMENTS

T his book has a long history. I began my research back in the 1960s while I was on the editorial staff at Our Sunday Visitor, using the fine library OSV had then. But in 1967 I was given business rather than editorial responsibilities — marketing manager, executive vice president, and then president and publisher — and I put the book aside.

When I returned to the editorial world in 1984 by becoming editor-in-chief of *The Criterion* of the Archdiocese of Indianapolis, I confined my writing to that newspaper (except for my first book). After my retirement from *The Criterion* at the end of 1996, I wrote other books, especially about saints. It wasn't until after the events of September 11, 2001, and the expressions of patriotism that flowed from them, that I was inspired to finish what had I started back in the 1960s.

Producing a book is always a team effort, and I want to express my appreciation to all those at Our Sunday Visitor who made this book possible, beginning with President and Publisher Greg Erlandson, who has always been most gracious to me through the years. The Editorial Development Manager, Jackie Lindsey, not only made helpful and valuable suggestions, but also supplied some resources to help me in my research for the chapter on Cardinal O'Connor. Darrin Malone, the project editor for the book, asked just the right questions to make sure I clarified some of the facts in the book and added a few facts about Archbishop Noll's mission-related activities.

The portraits that appear before each chapter were produced by Margaret Bunson, and I thank her also for her suggestion that I add three people to my final chapter on additional patriotic churchmen. I also greatly appreciate the design work of Sherri Hoffman for the interior of the book and of Troy Lefevra for the cover. And thank you, too, to Jill Kurtz for helping develop the book for marketing.

INTRODUCTION

Patriotism and Catholicism

D aniel Webster once said, "Whatever makes men good Christians, makes them good citizens." This book is about men who were both good Christians and good citizens; more specifically, they were good Catholics and good Americans.

The lives of these nine men span much of the history of our nation — from the Revolutionary War to the twentieth century. (It purposely does not include people living today.) Yet they all had a great deal in common. First and foremost, they all had a great love for their country and for their Church. They were all extremely proud of the principles underlying our Constitution, and all recognized the possibilities the Church had for growth under the American form of government. In addition, they were all vigorous defenders of their Church, particularly when it came to protecting the freedom of religion guaranteed by the Constitution.

These men were courageous to an unusual degree while fighting for the religious or political principles in which they believed. Whether it was Cardinal Gibbons praising the American principle of the separation of Church and State to the Church officials in Rome, Bishop England defending the rights of the Catholic Church before a joint session of Congress, or Archbishop Noll answering the charges of speakers at anti-Catholic meetings, they all spoke as frankly as they knew how.

And they did know how, for they were all outstanding speakers. This is one trait that stands out in everything written about each of these men — they were all exceptional orators. Undoubtedly, Archbishop Sheen had the largest audiences because he had a regular television show, but all of them attracted large crowds during their time.

They also were excellent and prolific writers. Four of them were journalists and editors: Bishop England, who founded the first Catholic newspaper in this country, *The Catholic Miscellany*; Archbishop Hughes, who founded and edited *The Catholic Herald* in Philadelphia before he was consecrated a bishop; Father Hecker, founder and editor of *The Catholic World*; and Archbishop Noll, founder and editor of *Our Sunday Visitor*. Although not an editor, Cardinal Gibbons was author of the all-time best-selling Catholic book, *Faith of Our Fathers*, which is rivaled in popularity only by Archbishop Noll's *Father Smith Instructs Jackson* — both of these works were instructional books widely used in convert classes for decades. Archbishop Sheen's books were also used to instruct converts.

———

That there would ever be American Catholic patriots such as these men must have seemed completely impossible in the year 1763. In that year the treaty was signed that ended the French and Indian War — and also ended, to all appearances at the time, any influence the Catholic Church would ever have in this country. By this treaty, all of eastern North America, with only a few minor exceptions, was placed under the control of England — and England at that time was decidedly unfriendly to the Catholic Church.

Catholicism arrived in America with Christopher Columbus, when he planted the cross on the tiny island of San Salvador in the Bahamas in 1492. He claimed the new land for the Catholic rulers of Spain, Ferdinand of Aragon and Isabella of Castile, who immediately planned for the evangelization of the country. For the next two hundred years, exploration and the spread of Catholicism went hand in hand as Spain added the territories they called Florida, New Mexico, and California to its empire.

In the meantime, France, another Catholic country, began exploring the country from the north, reaching into the Great Lakes. The North American martyrs (Jesuit missionaries from France martyred while laboring among American Indian tribes) wrote a brilliant chapter in the history of the Church in this country. Then Robert Cavalier de la Salle explored the Mississippi River, found its mouth in 1682, and took possession of the entire Mississippi valley for France.

Between the Spanish explorations to the south and the French explorations to the north were the English colonies along the eastern coast of the New World. The only "Catholic colony" was Maryland, a memorial to the Calvert family. It was founded as a religious haven for Catholics, who fled from persecutions in their homelands. It did not remain a Catholic colony for long, however, for Cecil Calvert made William Stone, an Episcopalian, the governor of Maryland in an attempt to gain the good will of the Protestants. Soon Maryland brought forth vicious anti-Catholic legislation, forbidding Catholics to attend Mass except privately in their own homes and disbarring them from all public offices.

In the peace of 1763, at the end of the French and Indian War, England won Florida from Spain in return for Cuba, which had been captured during the war. England also took from France all the territory east of the Mississippi, except New Orleans, which was conceded to Spain along with all of Louisiana west of the river.

Under England, the fate of the Catholic Church in the colonies was bleak indeed. There was considerable anti-Catholic sentiment throughout the colonies, and Catholics suffered under stringent penal laws. But then the founders of our country were wise enough to write the Declaration of Independence and later the Constitution, which guaranteed freedom of religion. Catholic leaders were wise enough to appreciate these great documents. For, as Archbishop Noll pointed out, "The philosophy of the Declaration of Independence is the philosophy of the Church."

Two centuries before Thomas Jefferson wrote the Declaration of Independence, Cardinal Robert Bellarmine, now a saint of the Church, wrote:

> Secular or civil power is instituted by men; it is in the people, unless they bestow it on a prince. This power is immediately in the whole multitude, as in the subject of it; for this power is in the divine law, but the divine law hath given this power to no particular man — if the positive law be taken away, there is left no reason why amongst a multitude (who are equal) one rather than another should bear rule over the rest. Power is given by the multitude to one man, or to more by the same law of nature; for the commonwealth cannot exercise this power; therefore, it is bound to bestow it upon some one man, or some few. It depends upon the consent of the multitude to ordain over themselves a king, or consul, or other magistrates; and if there be a lawful cause, the multitude may change the kingdom into an aristocracy or democracy.

In the same century (the sixteenth), Father Francisco Suarez, a Jesuit, was the chief champion of the rights of the people and the chief foe of the doctrine of the "divine right of kings." He taught that kings do not reign by divine right, but by the "expression of the multitude." Thus, only if a king, or emperor, or president, is placed in power with the consent of the multitude, is his right to rule under the sanction of God recognized.

That this was Catholic doctrine rather than Protestant is shown from this statement made by the University of Cambridge in 1688 in its address to King Charles II:

> We still believe and maintain that our kings derive not their title from the people but from God, that to Him only

they are accountable, that it belongs not to the subjects either to create or censure but to honor and obey their sovereign, who comes to be so by a fundamental hereditary right of succession which no religion, no law, no fault or forfeiture can alter or diminish.

This statement, made by a Protestant group, clearly shows that they did not accept the Catholic doctrine that a ruler reigns by the consent of the governed.

Writers on American democracy often trace its origin to the Magna Carta, drafted in England early in the thirteenth century. The Magna Carta was nothing more than a centuries-old Catholic conception, which Catholic barons demanded from an unwilling king.

In his encyclical on the Christian Constitution of States, *Immortale Dei*, Pope Leo XIII presented the Church's teachings most clearly concerning the relationship of spiritual and civil society:

God has divided the governments of mankind between two powers, ecclesiastical and civil; one presides over divine things, the other over human. Each in its sphere is sovereign; each is marked with limits perfectly defined, and traced in conformity with its nature, and its special end. Hence there is, as it were, a circumscribed sphere, in which each exercises its action *jure proprio*. At the same time, their authority being exercised on the same subject, it may happen that one and the same thing, though for different reasons, may come under the jurisdiction and judgment of both powers; ... hence the necessity of having between the two powers a system of well-ordered relations, analogous to that which in man constitutes the union of soul and body.

We can form a just idea of the nature and power of these relations only by considering the nature of each of these two powers and by bearing in mind the excellence and nobility of their ends, since the special and immediate end of one is the promotion of temporal interests, and of the other, spiritual and eternal interests. Thus all that is sacred in human things in any respect whatever, all that relates to the salvation of souls and the worship of God, either through its nature or through the relation of its end, comes under the authority of the Church. As to other things which relate to the civil and political order, it is just that they be subject to civil authority, for Christ has commanded us to "render therefore to Caesar the things that are Caesar's, and to God the things that are God's" (Matthew 22:21, RSV).

This teaching of the Church offers the greatest safeguards to the people, for no tyrant or dictator fits into the government of that sort of civil society; and no head of the Church will interfere with any civil ruler who keeps within the limits of his jurisdiction and tries to promote the temporal well-being of his subjects. There have been conflicts between Church and State in the past, but these took place only because kings and emperors and dictators insisted on being both ecclesiastical and civil rulers, or at least on running the Church.

The best historians agree that the difficulties between Church and State grew out of efforts made by civil rulers to subject the Church to the State, rather than from interference with State affairs by ecclesiastical rulers, unless the rights of God and of the people were attacked.

The Catholic Church actually contains many of the ideas which are vital to a democracy, as former President Woodrow Wilson pointed out. Referring to the Middle Ages, he wrote:

> The Roman Church was then, as it is now, a great democracy. There was no peasant so humble that he might not become pope of Christendom; and every chancellery in Europe, every court in Europe, was ruled by these learned, trained and accomplished men, the priesthood of that great and dominant body.

The leaders of the Catholic Church in the United States were, then, quite ready to agree with William Gladstone when he said, "The American Constitution is, so far as I can see, the most wonderful work ever struck off at a given time by the brain and purpose of man." The Catholic Church can be depended on to defend the democracy which our founding fathers set up.

Catholics have also defended this country whenever they have been called on to do so. In World War I, the war fought "to make the world safe for democracy," more than eight hundred thousand Catholics served in the military forces of the United States with a death toll of more than twenty-two thousand. And in World War II it was estimated that between twenty-five and thirty-five percent of the military personnel were Catholic — far beyond their proportion of the total population of the country. The number of Catholic chaplains was three thousand thirty-six, of whom eighty-three died in the course of the war.

———·———

Is there as much patriotism in the United States today as there was in the past? Before the terrorist attacks on September 11, 2001, it seemed that there was not. One simply did not hear the impassioned speeches praising democracy and our republic that were once prevalent, especially on national holidays. It seemed to be a sign of a lack of sophistication for a person to say that he loves his country and that he ardently believes in our democratic way of life. Since the events of September 11, 2001, however, there seems to have been an increase in patriotism.

Nevertheless, it seems that democracy is no longer taught in our schools to the extent that it once was. In many schools, it appears that the teaching of the fundamentals of democracy is as outlawed as teaching the fundamentals of religion.

This is not true in Catholic schools. There a love of country is taught at the same time as the truths of Catholicism. Patriotism is taught as a virtue, and the fact that "all men are created equal," which from its very language is a religious principle as well as a principle of democracy, is accepted by Catholic children just as readily as "two and two are four."

If for a long time there was less patriotism among Americans than there was while our country was growing up, it could be because it is difficult to teach the principles of democracy without teaching the fundamentals of religion. Difficult? It's impossible! For if you don't believe in a Creator who made all men equal and endowed them with "certain inalienable rights," you immediately deny the whole basis on which democracy rests.

Catholics should, therefore, be the greatest patriots in the United States. Many principles on which our country was founded are seen in Catholic doctrine. These principles are taught to our children in Catholic parochial schools while children in our public schools do not learn them adequately because it is forbidden to teach religion in those schools.

Therefore, if we are to preserve our country, it would seem essential that we return to the Christian order that once existed in the United States. The majority of our citizens are not receiving the knowledge of Christian principles that is necessary to return to that Christian order. This return can be effected only by re-creating a Christian public opinion through our schools and colleges, and through the press, radio, and television.

This is not advocating that our public schools teach a particular religion — hence there should be nothing unconstitutional involved. But if we are to preserve our Constitution, it is essential that the schools teach those religious fundamentals that are basic to all religions.

———

American Catholics have a right to be proud of the men whose stories are told in the following pages. They should have pride not only that their co-religionists demonstrated such outstanding patriotism, but also that their country could produce leaders of their

Church of such great caliber. These Catholic patriots should be an inspiration to all Americans, particularly Catholic Americans. We need this kind of inspiration in today's world.

Archbishop John Carroll

I presume that your fellow citizens will not forget the patriotic part which you took in the accomplishment of their Revolution and the establishment of your government.

— *GEORGE WASHINGTON TO ARCHBISHOP JOHN CARROLL*

CHAPTER 1

-•◦•-

Archbishop John Carroll

The four men who disembarked from a boat in Montreal, Quebec, on April 29, 1776, were a weary group of travelers. They had been traveling for over a month, and in those days traveling was tedious. It was particularly tiring for one of the four, Benjamin Franklin, as he was seventy years old.

The other three men were Samuel Chase, Charles Carroll of Carrollton, and the Rev. John Carroll. They were on an official mission from the fledgling government of the United States to the people of Canada — a mission that was doomed to failure.

Canada was considered an extremely important factor in the military and political planning of both the United States and England during the Revolutionary War. At the beginning, the colonists enjoyed considerable success militarily, as General Montgomery's troops managed to capture Montreal on November 18, 1775. Seven weeks later, however, Montgomery was killed while leading a heroic assault on Quebec.

While the fighting was taking place, the Continental Congress decided it was imperative to put the American cause in a good light to the people of Canada. So, on February 15, 1776, it passed a resolution appointing a commission of three — Benjamin Franklin, Samuel Chase, and Charles Carroll — to go to Canada to try to gain the support of the Canadian people. In addition to these three, the Congress resolved that Charles Carroll prevail on Father John Carroll, his cousin (although not a first cousin), to accompany them "to assist them in such matters as they shall think useful."

Father Carroll was asked to go because it was known that he was a faithful patriot and because religion was of prime importance in these negotiations. Although Canada was under British sovereignty, it formed a land apart from the colonies because it had come into British hands only in 1763 at the end of the French and Indian War. Prior to that time it had been under French rule. Since most of the residents were French in nationality, and hence Catholic, Canada had managed to win religious freedom from England through the Quebec Act, passed by the British Parliament in 1774.

This act said:

> His Majesty's subjects, professing the religion of the Church of Rome, of and in the province of Quebec, may have, hold, and enjoy the free exercise of the religion of the Church of Rome, subject to the King's supremacy ... and the clergy of the said Church may hold, receive, and enjoy their accustomed dues and rights with respect to such persons only as shall profess the said religion.

This act created extremely bitter feelings among the colonists and must be considered a primary cause of the Revolutionary War. John Jay pictured Catholics as helping England enslave America through the act. The Continental Congress itself, in an address to Great Britain, stated:

> Nor can we suppress our astonishment that a British Parliament should ever consent to establish in that country (Canada) a religion that has deluged your island with blood, and dispersed impiety, bigotry, persecution, murder, and rebellion through every part of the world.

On October 26, 1774, the Congress protested to England's King George III against "establishing an absolute government and the

Roman Catholick [sic] religion throughout those vast regions that border the westerly and northerly boundaries of the free Protestant English settlements."

There is no doubt that the members of the Continental Congress were a bit two-faced. On the same day they protested to George III against freedom of religion for the Catholics in Canada, they wrote to the Canadians:

> We are all too well-acquainted with the liberality of sentiment distinguishing your nation to imagine that difference of religion will prejudice you against a hearty amity with us. You know that the transcendent nature of freedom elevates those who united in her cause above all such low-minded infirmities.

The Canadian people, however, were not unaware of the real attitude of the Continental Congress toward their religion. Yet this same Congress had the gall to send a commission to Canada to seek their help in the war against the country that so recently had granted religious rights to Canadian Catholics. It's no wonder that the Congress wanted Father Carroll and Charles Carroll, the most noted Catholics in the United States, to be a part of that commission.

It should be pointed out, though, that the Quebec Act did far more than recognize and protect the Catholic religion in Quebec (as Canada was then known). It gave to Quebec a large amount of territory, westward to the Mississippi River and southward to the Ohio River. The protection of the Catholic religion was not really out of sympathy for the Catholics (or why would not Britain have done the same for Catholics living in Ireland and Great Britain itself?). No, the Quebec Act was passed deliberately to provoke antagonism between England and the United States. This didn't affect the feelings of the Catholics of Canada, however, who could take advantage of the provisions of the Quebec Act and who knew only too well how the United States felt toward Catholicism.

It is really somewhat of a mystery why Catholics in the United States took part in the rebellion against England. They could, after all, expect better treatment from Great Britain than they could expect from the new government of the United States. England showed this through the Quebec Act, while some of the manifestations of bigotry were at their height in the colonies. It was only in Maryland, Virginia, Pennsylvania, and Delaware that penal laws against Catholics had been swept away.

An example of the bigotry of the people at the time of the Revolutionary War was the celebration of "Pope Day." On this day, an effigy of the pope was carried in mockery through the streets and then burned. George Washington, to whom this insult to Catholics was distasteful, abolished "Pope Day," the 1774 celebrations being the last.

One might wonder how Father Carroll thought he could support the United States, considering the attitude its citizens had toward his religion. Father Carroll, and Charles Carroll, too, thought that the hostility of the colonists to the Catholic Faith was actually foreign to the American character, and that with the growing power of the colonies and the spread of correct knowledge about the Catholic Church, Catholicism would eventually come to be regarded in its true light.

Father Carroll reveals in his letters that the request of the Continental Congress that he accompany the commission created a difficult decision for him. He acknowledged that the Congress had done him "the distinguished and unexpected honor" of asking him to go with the commission, but he did not feel that he had the right to ask Canada to do more for the United States than to maintain neutrality. He did not believe that Canada would be morally justified in making war on England. "They have not the same motives for taking up arms against England which render the resistance of the other colonies so justifiable," he wrote. Although the letters do not definitely so state, he presumably agreed to accompany the commission with the private understanding that he would plead only for Canada to remain neutral.

The commission began the journey in March of 1776 and arrived in Montreal on April 29. Once there, it was immediately apparent that the mission was hopeless. Because of the statements by Congress regarding the Canadians and their religion, the clergy, headed by Bishop Jean Briand, were quite hostile. By May 12, Father Carroll and Benjamin Franklin had left to return home. Charles Carroll and Samuel Chase remained to try to carry on the mission.

During this trip, particularly while returning, Father Carroll and Benjamin Franklin struck up a friendship. Franklin was ailing on the return trip and appreciated Father Carroll's aid. He wrote to Chase and Charles Carroll while they were still in Canada, "I find I grow daily more feeble, and I think I could hardly have got along so far but for Mr. Carroll's friendly assistance and tender care of me." (At that time it was customary among non-Catholics to refer to priests as *Mister*.) Brantz Mayer wrote that "Franklin did not forget the kind attentions of the Rev. John Carroll during his journey; nor did he fail to appreciate the virtues and intellectual cultivation of that excellent gentleman."

———

Just as George Washington is known as the father of our country, so John Carroll is the father of the Catholic Church in the United States. Father Carroll was elected (yes, elected) the first bishop in the United States on March 25,1789, in a solemn conclave of the priests of the United States at Whitemarsh, Maryland. Slightly more than a month later, Washington took the oath of office to become the first president of the United States — on April 30, 1789.

Although the Church in the United States received its first bishop at the same time the country received its first president, the Church was officially established five years earlier, on June 9, 1784, when Father John Carroll was appointed prefect apostolic for the territory coterminous with the new republic. Before making this appointment, the papal nuncio wrote to Benjamin Franklin, then the United States ambassador to France, requesting permission do so. Franklin forwarded the message to the Continental Congress, which directed him to answer:

The subject of his application to Dr. Franklin being purely spiritual, it is without the jurisdiction and powers of Congress who have no authority to permit or refuse it, these powers being reserved to the several states individually.

As Rev. John Courtney Murray, a Jesuit, observed in his book *We Hold These Truths*:

The good nuncio must have been happily surprised on receiving this communication. Not for centuries had the Holy See been free to erect a bishopric and appoint a bishop without the prior consent of government, without proper exercise of government's right of presentation, without all the legal formalities with which the so-called Catholic states had fettered the freedom of the Church. In the United States the freedom of the Church was completely unfettered. She could organize herself with a full independence which is her native right.

The Holy See's first thought was to appoint a bishop in 1784. Father Carroll, however, advised against doing so because he felt that such an appointment would be resented by the United States citizens as an undue interference in their affairs and an unwarranted show of power by foreigners. He wrote:

The jealousy in our government of the interference of any foreign jurisdiction is known to be such that we cannot expect, in my opinion, ought not to wish, that they would tolerate any other than that which being purely spiritual, is essential to our religion, to wit, an acknowledgement of the pope's spiritual supremacy.

Father Carroll, therefore, was named prefect apostolic in a letter dated June 9, 1784, from Cardinal Antonelli, the prefect of the Sacred Congregation of Propaganda. This letter acknowledges the friendship between Father Carroll and Franklin, for it contains the clause, "Since it is known that your appointment will please and gratify many citizens of your republic, particularly Mr. Franklin, the eminent person who represents the same republic at the court of the Most Christian King [the king of France]."

Father Carroll was not anxious to accept the appointment as prefect apostolic, even though he, more than any other priest, had been responsible for organizing the Church in the United States. He realized the many implications involved in the appointment, and accepted the appointment only because his friends feared that a refusal might put them under a European prelate. He did not send his formal acceptance until January 19, 1785.

In his letter of acceptance, he again mentioned the problem of foreign interference in the affairs of the Church in the United States. He told Cardinal Antonelli, "The Catholics desire that no pretext be given to the enemies of our religion to accuse us of depending unnecessarily on a foreign authority."

In time, however, it became apparent that a prefect apostolic did not have sufficient authority to settle many of the problems of organizing the Church. This could obviously be done efficiently only by one who had the backing of episcopal consecration. Yet the American priests still feared the public's adverse reaction to a bishop appointed by the Holy See. Father Carroll insisted that any American bishop "must be a diocesan bishop, and his appointment must come neither from His Holiness, for that would create more jealousy in our government than even in France, Germany, or Spain, nor from the assemblies of different executives ... but he should be chosen by the Catholic clergy themselves."

Cardinal Antonelli proposed to Pope Pius VI, therefore, that the priests of the United States be permitted, "at least on this first occasion," to elect their own bishop. The pope agreed to this arrangement and ordered that it be carried out. The priests of the United States, therefore, met at Whitemarsh, requested to have Baltimore as the episcopal city, and elected Father Carroll as their choice for the first bishop of the United States.

———

John Carroll was born on January 8, 1735, to Daniel and Eleanor Carroll at Upper Marlboro, Maryland, and received his early education in his own home. Then, as many Catholic boys did in those days, he and his cousin Charles risked the indictment of the penal laws, which forbade Catholics to send their children to foreign schools, by traveling to St. Omer in France. After studying at St. Omer for several years, Charles Carroll continued his studies in England while John joined the Jesuits. He was ordained to the priesthood in 1769 after studying at Liege, Belgium. After his ordination, he taught in Flanders for four years and then served as chaplain to Lord Arundel in England.

In 1773, the Holy See suppressed the Society of Jesus as an organization and ordered the individual members to express their acceptance of the suppression in writing. Father Carroll did so and then decided to return to America because he could foresee the Revolutionary War and was resolved to cast his lot with America. He returned in 1774.

Upon returning, Father Carroll built a mission church at his mother's home at Rock Creek, Maryland, and served the Catholic population of that area and of nearby Virginia. He devoted himself to this work until the Continental Congress asked him to undertake the mission to Canada. It was from this mission that he first gained his reputation as a patriot. It also gave him a certain prominence among his brother priests.

It was Father Carroll who first realized the difficulties the Church in the United States faced in regard to jurisdiction. Until 1773, most of the priests in this country were Jesuits. There were twenty-four priests in Maryland and Pennsylvania at that time, and they were all Jesuits. Hence they were under the jurisdiction of the Society of Jesus. When this society was suppressed in 1773, the priests were supposed to be subject to the local ordinary. For the priests in the United States, that was Bishop Richard Challoner, vicar apostolic of London, England.

During the Revolutionary War, communications with England were naturally cut off, and Bishop Challoner would have nothing to do with the rebelling Americans. When he died in 1781, his successor, Bishop James Talbot, refused jurisdiction over the former colonies and refused to grant faculties to two priests who were returning to the United States.

Father Carroll recognized this as a serious problem, so he proposed a plan of organization to the other American priests. Father John Lewis, who had been the superior of the American priests when they were Jesuits, called a meeting of the priests at Whitemarsh to consider Father Carroll's plan. At this meeting, a constitution was prepared and a petition drawn up to the Holy See requesting a regularly constituted ecclesiastical organization. As we have seen, the Holy See responded favorably to the request and appointed Father Carroll prefect apostolic.

———•———

Just as the government of the United States had a difficult time achieving an efficient government (the Declaration of Independence was signed in 1776 and the Articles of Confederation were drafted in 1777, but the articles were not ratified until 1781; then work began on the Constitution in 1787; it was ratified in 1788, and George Washington was elected and inaugurated in 1789), so the Church in the United States had a precarious time. When one considers the task that was Carroll's as father of the Catholic Church in the United States and the accomplishments made during his lifetime, the man's administrative ability must be rated as utterly fantastic.

When he first became prefect apostolic in 1785, there were about twenty-five thousand Catholics among the four million inhabitants of America, and most of these — Carroll figured about fifteen thousand eight hundred — lived in Maryland. Twenty years later, there were seventy thousand Catholics in America.

Of the Catholics living in America in 1785, the fifteen thousand eight hundred Catholics in Maryland had nineteen priests to serve them; the seven thousand in Pennsylvania had five priests; the one thousand five hundred in New York and the two hundred in Virginia had no resident priests; and this was about the extent of Catholicism along the Atlantic seaboard. Bishop Carroll admitted that he had no way of knowing exactly how many Catholics were living beyond the Allegheny Mountains, but they were being cared for only by the veteran missionary Father Peter Gibault.

Compare this with the status of the Church in America when Archbishop Carroll died in 1815: There was an archbishopric and four suffragan sees (New York, Philadelphia, Boston, and Bardstown, Kentucky), and another diocese had been erected beyond the Mississippi River. The Archdiocese of Baltimore had theological seminaries, a novitiate and scholasticate, colleges, convents, academies, schools, and a religious community devoted to education and the works of mercy.

In Pennsylvania, there were priests and churches through the mountain districts all the way to Pittsburgh. In New York, Catholics were increasing numerically west of Albany. In New England, the Faith was steadily gaining under the leadership of Bishop John Cheverus. There were churches and priests in all the large cities from Boston to Augusta and westward to St. Louis and New Orleans, with many other churches in smaller towns. Altogether, there were more than one hundred churches and priests.

It is impossible here to show how Bishop Carroll was able to manage this tremendous growth of the Church. We must let a brief outline suffice:

Bishop Carroll recognized that the American Church's biggest need was for priests. There were only twenty-five priests in the diocese (which comprised all of the United States at that time, the country east of the Mississippi River except Florida) and many of them were elderly. The bishop established a seminary and brought the Sulpicians to this country from France to teach in the seminary. The first seminarians arrived May 29, 1792. The first ordination took place in 1793, and the new priest, Father Stephen Badin, was sent to the Kentucky missions where he spent a long, arduous, and extremely fruitful life.

In 1791, Bishop Carroll invited the priests to the first synod in the United States. This synod adopted the first body of laws for governing the Church in this country.

The first coadjutor bishop to Bishop Carroll was Father Lawrence Graessel, but he died before he could be consecrated, so Carroll then selected Father Leonard Neale, who was appointed by the pope in 1795. In 1805 Carroll became administrator of the Diocese of Louisiana and Florida after the United States purchased those territories from France. Later, this diocese was confided to the care of Bishop William Du Bourg.

Bishop Carroll laid the cornerstone of his cathedral on July 7, 1806. On April 8, 1808, the four suffragan dioceses were erected and Baltimore was named an archiepiscopal see with Carroll as archbishop.

———

Most importantly, by the time of the archbishop's death in 1815, Catholics, who had lately again shown their patriotism during the War of 1812, were free! Carroll was largely responsible for this program, too. He was quick to speak out when the Church was attacked — and that was often in those days. Although not as vigorous a defender of the Faith as Bishop England or Archbishop Hughes (as we shall see in the chapters about those men), he did speak out when the patriotism of Catholics was questioned.

An example of this was his reply, under the pen name of "Pacificus," to a letter that appeared in the May 9, 1789, issue of the *Gazette of the United States* that questioned Catholics' loyalty to the United States. Bishop Carroll stated that the first letter must have been painful to "every friend to the rights of conscience, equal liberty, and diffusive happiness." He then claimed that the writer was one of those who think it consistent with justice to exclude certain citizens from the honors and emoluments of society merely on account of their religious opinions ... If such be his views, in vain then have Americans associated into one great union, under the express condition of not being shackled by religious tests.

Carroll then went on to tell how Catholics had fought for the United States during the Revolutionary War. He wrote that their blood "had flowed as freely (in proportion to their numbers) to cement the fabric of independence, as that of any of their fellow citizens. They concurred with perhaps greater unanimity than any other body of men in recommending and promoting that government from whose influence America anticipates all the blessings of justice, peace, plenty, good order, and civil religious liberty."

Bishop Carroll not only defended Catholics' patriotism, he also did what he could to ensure that Catholics always retained that virtue. As historian Theodore Roemer wrote, "Carroll kept insisting that the children of the Church put no obstacles in the way of democracy, and that they always conduct themselves both as true democrats and as loyal Catholics."

———

The first American bishop and the first American president had a deep respect for each other. Of this fact we have the testimony of George Washington Parke Custis, the adopted son of George Washington. Custis wrote:

> You are pleased to ask me whether the late Dr. Carroll was in intimate acquaintance of Washington. He was more, sir. From his exalted worth as a minister of God, his stainless character as a man, and above all his distinguished service as a patriot of the Revolution, Dr. Carroll stood high, very high, in the esteem of the *Pater Patriae*.

This esteem was reciprocated. Bishop Carroll once praised "the firmness, the undaunted courage, the personal influence, and consummate prudence of that wonderful man, our President Washington." When Washington was inaugurated, Bishop-elect Carroll and four other prominent Catholics — Charles and Daniel Carroll (John Carrol's cousin and older brother, respectively), Dominick Lynch, and Thomas Fitzsimons — presented to the president an address of congratulations, "because we conceive that no human means are so available to promote the welfare of the United States as the prolongation of your health and life, in which are included the energy of your example, the wisdom of your counsels, and the persuasive eloquence of your virtues."

President Washington responded with an acknowledgement of the role Catholics played in the fight for independence and a hope that the people of the United States would realize "that all those who conduct themselves as worthy members of the community are equally entitled to the protection of civil government." He went on to say:

> I presume that your fellow citizens will not forget the patriotic part which you took in the accomplishment of their Revolution, and the establishment of your Government: or the important assistance which they received from a nation in which the Roman Catholic Faith is professed [a reference to the help received from France].

Other people recognized the esteem in which the father of our country and the father of the Catholic Church in the United States held each other. Because of this, Archbishop Carroll was invited to officiate at the laying of the cornerstone of the Washington Monument on July 4, 1815. Unfortunately, however, he had to decline the invitation — and declining the invitation turned out to be his last public act before his death. He felt impelled to decline the invitation, he said, because "at my advanced period of life, and with a half-extinguished voice, I must inevitably fall so much below the solemnity of the occasion and public expectation that respect for the super-eminent Washington, and for my fellow citizens, compels me to offer my excuse to the committee."

———

Archbishop Carroll was a friend to many of the early leaders of our country, and they all had a deep respect for his high intelligence and for his patriotism. His personality was such that he commanded the confidence of Protestants as well as Catholics, and this was no mean accomplishment in those days when the Catholic Church was so little regarded. The private letters of two non-Catholics, one a former secretary of state and the other a former secretary of war, are revealing in this regard. On June 9, 1813, Timothy Pickering wrote to James McHenry:

> The day before yesterday I met Bishop Carroll, with the fine, calm, composed, but cheerful countenance which distinguishes that good man. He mentioned with tender affection and regret the situation of "my friend McHenry." [McHenry was then an invalid.] There is a charm in the manners, and especially the face, of Bishop Carroll, of which I have rarely if ever seen the equal.

McHenry replied:

> I can safely say from a long and social intercourse with him that the benignity which you describe as appearing so strikingly in his countenance is not greater than the real benignity of his heart.

———

When Archbishop Carroll was on his deathbed, members of his clergy were in an adjoining room discussing how to give the last rites to someone of the archbishop's exalted rank. Requiring a book that was in the archbishop's room, one of the priests quietly went in to get it. But Archbishop Carroll heard the man enter, called him to his bed, told him that he was aware of what he was looking for, and directed him to a particular shelf where he would find the book.

The archbishop then expressed a wish to be laid on the floor to die. After this was done, he asked to have the *Miserere* read, following it with great devotion. Then, obviously knowing that he was about to die, and seeing his sister and other weeping relatives about, he asked if a conveyance was prepared to take them away after his death. After being assured that there was, he told those gathered that the scene was about to close, gave them all his blessing, turned his head to the side, and died.

———

In 1889, one hundred years after Archbishop Carroll was appointed the first U.S. bishop, the centenary of the event was celebrated in Baltimore with great pomp and ceremony. At that time, Cardinal James Gibbons praised Archbishop Carroll for having laid the foundations of civic and religious cooperation. He said in part:

> The calm judgment of posterity recognizes John Carroll as a providential agent in molding the diverse elements in the United States into an organized Church. He did not wish the Church to vegetate as a delicate exotic plant; he wished it to become a sturdy tree, deep-rooted in the soil, to grow with the growth and bloom with the development of the country, inured to its climate, braving its storms, and invigorated by them, and yielding abundantly the fruits of sanctification.

He praised "the civic and moral virtues" of Archbishop Carroll and also Bishop Cheverus, Bishop Flaget, Archbishop Hughes, and

Bishop England, but warned that they "will be a reproach to us, if we have no share in their patriotism and piety."

———•———

This chapter about Archbishop John Carroll should not be closed without an additional word about his cousin, Charles Carroll of Carrollton, who was one of the most ardent patriots in the early history of the United States. He undoubtedly was the most influential Catholic of this period of American history. The wealthiest man in the colonies, he was the only Catholic to sign the Declaration of Independence. But he had more than that to his credit.

Born in Annapolis, Maryland, on September 19, 1737, Charles was educated in France along with his cousin John, who was two years his elder. After studying law in London for several years, he returned to this country in 1765 to take over an estate at Carrollton, Maryland. He wrote in the *Maryland Gazette* against taxation without representation, which was to become a battle cry of the Revolutionary War, and, in 1774, he was elected to the provincial convention even though Catholics were disenfranchised. He served on the committee to arm the state, manufacture gunpowder, and, as we have seen, to seek aid from Canada.

He successfully swung a hostile Maryland government to approve a move toward independence supported by the Continental Congress. He was elected to the Continental Congress in 1776 and risked more than most colonists, because of his large fortune, when he signed the Declaration of Independence.

After the Revolutionary War, Charles was elected a United States senator from Maryland. He was an ardent supporter of George Washington and the Federalist Party. In 1792, when a new law made it impossible to hold two political posts at the same time, he resigned as a United States senator to retain his position as a state senator. He served his state in that capacity until 1801.

His last years were spent in political retirement, though he continued to comment on public events, and, since he was the last surviving signer of the Declaration of Independence, he was highly esteemed throughout the country. He died at the age of ninety-five on November 14, 1832.

———

Still another member of the Carroll family was an active patriot during the early years of the United States. Daniel Carroll, Archbishop Carroll's older brother, served as a member of the Continental Congress from 1780 to 1784, was a delegate to the Constitutional Convention in Philadelphia in 1789, and was one of the signers of the United States Constitution.

He was a member of the national Congress from 1789 to 1791 and one of three commissioners appointed to lay out the site of the capital in Washington, D.C. He himself donated a quarter of the land for the capital.

He too lived to an old age, dying in 1829 at the age of ninety-six. Indeed, Charles and Daniel Carroll made Archbishop John Carroll appear to die early in life, since he "only" lived to age eighty — dying one month before his eighty-first birthday.

Bishop John England

I would not allow to the pope, or to any bishop of our
Church outside this Union, the smallest interference with
the humblest vote at our most insignificant balloting box.

— *BISHOP JOHN ENGLAND*

CHAPTER 2

——— ❖ ———

Bishop John England

On January 8, 1826, a thirty-nine-year-old man with strong, manly features, long sideburns but clean-shaven elsewhere, a broad, high forehead, and long auburn hair, stepped up to the speaker's rostrum in the United States House of Representatives. History was being made, for this was the first time a Catholic clergyman had ever spoken before the legislature of the United States.

Crowds had gathered for hours before the time set for the speech, and the chamber of the House of Representatives was packed for this momentous occasion. It was so packed, in fact, that it was reported that President John Quincy Adams found it difficult to get in, and, once in, much more difficult to find a seat. (There was no Secret Service in those days, and presidents often had to fend for themselves.) But Adams did get in, because he, more than any other man, wanted to hear what Bishop John England of Charleston, South Carolina, had to say. For Bishop England, although in this country only five years, already had the reputation of being a courageous and brilliant defender of the Catholic Faith. And at this point in the history of the Catholic Church in the United States, the Church needed a strong defender.

John Quincy Adams, himself a great orator and a man of courage when it came to standing up for the things in which he believed, unfortunately also ranks among the really great anti-Catholic leaders in the history of the United States. Considering his high rank and influence, he had done the Catholic Church considerable harm.

41

One of his orations in particular, delivered July 4, 1821, in Washington, contrasted freedom of religion and American democracy with "that pretentious system of despotism and superstition which, in the name of the meek and humble Jesus, has been spread over the Christian world." Adams was then secretary of state under President James Monroe.

Bishop England first met Adams in October of 1821, when England called on President Monroe and Adams in Washington. England was then on an informative tour of the eastern seaboard of the United States, for he had only arrived in the United States on December 30 of the previous year, and he wanted to learn as much about his new country as possible. Bishop England did not, of course, answer his host's Fourth of July assault while on his courtesy call, but undoubtedly hoped for the opportunity to do so publicly sometime in the future.

This opportunity came on Christmas Day, 1825, when Bishop England was again in Washington. He met the Adams speech point by point. But now, of course, he was retorting to the President of the United States rather than the secretary of state. It was this Christmas Day sermon which brought the invitation to address Congress.

Although he was one of the most eloquent preachers history has ever known, he undoubtedly felt that butterfly flutter in his breast as he began his address. He himself admitted later that he "had some unusual sensation of heart, and some unwonted glow in my cheek and on my forehead." For never before had there been such an opportunity for a representative of the Catholic Church to state that Church's position. And what an audience! It was composed of the lawmakers of the nation, most of whom had been nurtured in the anti-Catholic tradition of the time. And, of course, there was also the President of the United States himself, a man with whom he had already disagreed.

These men, for some perhaps the first and only time in their lives, were going to hear Catholic doctrine expounded by one who has been described as "courageous enough to speak the truth, zealous enough to try to break down the barriers of ignorance and prejudice standing between him and them, and eloquent enough to deliver his thoughts in such glowing language as to hold their attention to his message."

And speak he did. For two hours Bishop John England tried to give the American lawmakers a true picture of what the Catholic Church teaches, emphasizing the relations of the Church to the State and the State to the Church. He told them that he meant to answer the two burning questions of the day: "Can a free government possibly exist with the Roman Catholic religion?" and, "Can a good Roman Catholic be a loyal American citizen?"

He said:

> I would not allow to the pope, or to any bishop of our Church outside this Union, the smallest interference with the humblest vote at our most insignificant balloting box. If that tribunal which is established by the Creator to testify to me what he has revealed ... shall presume to go beyond that boundary which circumscribes its power, its acts are invalid; my rights are not to be destroyed by its usurpation; and there is no principle of my creed which prevents my using my natural rights in proper resistance to any tyrannical usurpation.

He told the president and the Congress, "You have no power to interfere with my religious rights," and added in the same breath, "The tribunal of the Church has no power to interfere with my civil rights."

———•———

John England loved his adopted country, the United States. (He received his U.S. citizenship papers less than a month after his speech before Congress.) In later years, he was to defend the United States against Europeans as vigorously as he defended the Catholic Church against Americans. And the Church needed defending in those days, for, although the Constitution guaranteed Catholics freedom of religion, most Americans had been so indoctrinated in anti-Catholic prejudice that freedom of religion was easier preached than put into actual practice.

Bishop England had made a reputation as a courageous defender of the Faith before he was made the first bishop of Charleston in 1820. Indeed, he must have been well-known to the Holy See to be appointed a bishop at the age of thirty-three and to be sent to a part of the United States where Catholics were hated with as much vehemence as anywhere in the country.

He had made his reputation in his native Ireland, where he was ordained, after being granted a special dispensation, at the age of twenty-two. (A man is supposed to be at least twenty-four before he can be ordained a priest.) His first assignments were in Cork, where he soon acquired national repute as a fearless fighter for Irish rights against the British.

Bishop England was later made pastor of a parish in Bandon, Ireland. The town boasted a sign above its gates that read, "Turk, Jew, or Atheist May Enter Here; But Not a Papist." In three years, Father England succeeded in removing the prejudice, bigotry, and intolerance for which the city was noted, and brought together the Catholics and Protestants in a bond of social and civic brotherhood.

Then, in 1820, he was appointed the first bishop of Charleston. After a long and extremely difficult voyage across the Atlantic Ocean, he stepped ashore in Charleston on December 30, 1820.

———

At the time Bishop England arrived in Charleston, James Monroe was nearing the end of his first term as president of the United States. The population of the United States was listed as 9,638,453, less than 100,000 of whom were Catholics. The Diocese of Charleston, which included the present states of North Carolina, South Carolina, and Georgia, had 1,482,559 people, according to the latest census, of whom it was estimated about 3,600 were Catholics "of a kind" — baptized Catholic, but not much more. The city of Charleston itself had about a thousand Catholics, but only a very few practicing Catholics, in a population of 37,555. Of these 37,555 people, 19,451 were black slaves, 3,146 were free black people, and 14,958 were white.

The new bishop spent most of the year 1821 visiting his diocese and a great deal of the rest of the United States in order to learn all he possibly could about the conditions he was to face. His travels to Baltimore, Philadelphia, New York and other cities acquainted him with the workings of the Protestant mind in the United States.

He soon learned that the American people were generally extremely ignorant of Catholic doctrine. He discovered, as he was later to write, that Protestants honestly believed that Catholic teaching and practice included: absolution of sins could be obtained for money; permission could be procured under the name of indulgence to perpetrate future crimes of the most atrocious nature at an exceedingly moderate charge; the principle that no faith was to be kept with heretics; that kings or princes who were not minions of the pope should be deposed and put to death; that all persons who were not members of the Catholic Church and consequently slaves to Rome would be exterminated whenever the opportunity was presented — these and a variety of similar accusations were held to be the true features of Popery.

Against these attacks on the Catholic Church, Bishop England found no defenses. There was not one paper in the entire country dedicated to the service of the Catholic Church, while there were many anti-Catholic publications.

It cannot be said of Bishop England that he was one to vacillate. After observing, during his tour of the United States in 1821, that there was a great need for a Catholic paper which could defend the Church, be began to plan just such a paper in February of 1822. On June 5, 1822, the first issue of the *United States Catholic Miscellany* was published, the first Catholic newspaper in the United States.

The *Miscellany* had a tough road ahead of it. Twice Bishop England had to discontinue its publication for lack of support. But finally, in July, 1826, it took a firm hold and lived on to carry to the world the message of John England until well past his death in 1842. It was the leading Catholic publication in the country until 1861, when it ended during the Civil War.

———

It was in the pages of the *Miscellany*, as well as in his numerous sermons, that Bishop England not only defended the Catholic Church, but also defended the American principles of freedom. For he was a true patriot. Bishop England fully understood what the United States Constitution meant and was convinced that its writers actually had built better than they knew when they decreed, "Congress shall make no law respecting the establishment of religion, or prohibiting the free exercise thereof." He realized that the Catholic Church would be able to grow in this atmosphere, and he was proud of the American people who ratified the Constitution, even if, mainly out of ignorance, they did not always practice what they preached.

Bishop England also defended the American way of life in the face of European detractors. Four times between 1832 and 1841, he journeyed to Europe to search for funds and personnel for his diocese, and, as would be expected from a man of the bishop's temperament, he attracted quite a reputation throughout Europe as a defender of Americanism.

During his first trip in 1832, he was in Rome when word arrived of the death of Charles Carroll of Carrollton, the only Catholic to sign the Declaration of Independence and the last of the signers to die. Bishop England took the occasion to preach a sermon in the Church of St. Isidore. He praised the signers of the Declaration, sketched the history of the Constitution and our federative system, and expostulated the principles of democracy.

Europe at that time still had not taken gracefully to the ideas of government exemplified in the United States, and the sermon made news throughout Rome. A distorted version was reported to the Holy Office, which conducted an investigation in search of possible heresy. There was no heresy, of course, and the investigation ended in England's favor.

The agitation stirred up by Bishop England's oration brought him in close contact with Pope Gregory XVI, who was not slow in recognizing the bishop's worth. The pope made Bishop England an assistant to the Pontifical Throne, and as such attended the Holy Father at Mass in the Vatican on Easter Sunday.

———

Pope Gregory also had other plans for the courageous and resourceful bishop of Charleston. He appointed England legate to Haiti, where trouble had been brewing for some time and the Church needed a man who understood the mentality of the black inhabitants and who would also be courageous enough to be firm regarding the interests of religion.

England did not want to accept this position because, as he pointed out to the pope, he was the bishop of a diocese that accepted black slavery and would not be accepted by a black republic that was proclaiming the rights of blacks. A series of revolutions, civil war, and attempts to oust religion were occurring in Haiti. The Holy Father, however, overruled England's objections and appointed him legate.

Bishop England devoted a great deal of time to this assignment — time that he begrudged because he felt that he should be working for his diocese. He was not completely successful in his efforts in Haiti. However, his work as legate so impressed Church authorities in the Vatican that rumors were ripe throughout Rome and Ireland, England's native country, that he was soon to be made a cardinal. Indeed, the *Dublin Register* prematurely announced, "We understand that the celebrated bishop of Charleston has been appointed cardinal by the pope." A later dispatch from Rome to the same publication stated, "Dr. England's promotion has been deferred, as his services are too valuable to the Church just at this moment."

Bishop England himself, however, had no desire to receive his "promotion." All he wanted was to be relieved of his assignment as legate so he could resume his duties as bishop of Charleston. Here is how he said it:

It was my intention to relieve myself altogether from this commission, for the purpose of being able to devote myself exclusively to the duties of my diocese. I besought His Holiness that, as by custom, those powers should cease upon my arrival at the Holy See [returning from Haiti], and they should not be renewed.

Pope Gregory disagreed and kept Bishop England as his legate to Haiti for a while longer. England wrote that he felt "grateful to our venerable chief pastor for the confidence he was kind enough to repose in me," but still felt that the termination of these duties "would be a relief."

At this time many of Bishop England's friends in both Rome and Ireland were trying to get the red hat for him. They were also trying to get him transferred from Charleston to Rome, for they felt that his talents and genius were being wasted in a diocese that had such a small Catholic population. But England wanted none of that. "An American citizen by choice and from adoption," he wrote, "I feel it to be my duty to contribute my humble efforts to sustain the character of our country."

"In that sentence," wrote Rev. John L. O'Brien in his book *John England, Bishop of Charleston: The Apostle to Democracy*, "John England gives his own interpretation of his vocation." O'Brien wrote that Bishop England did not care to be great in Rome, and he did not want to renew his fame in Ireland. Instead, he preferred to cast his lot with the struggling Church in the United States and to do his best to plant the Faith in a land founded on the principles of liberty. "He sensed truly the destiny of these United States, and he visioned the march of democracy down the ages," wrote O'Brien. "Europe did not need him, but the United States did."

———

The concern Bishop England expressed about being appointed legate to a black nation since he was bishop in a slave state proved to be well-founded. He soon found himself in the middle of the slavery problem that was then raging through the United States.

Northern abolitionists tried to show that the Catholic Church was on their side in this dispute, particularly after an encyclical on "The Slave Trade," by Pope Gregory XVI, appeared early in 1840. The issue achieved national importance in that year because it was an election year — the notorious Van Buren-Harrison campaign — and William Henry Harrison had the distinction of being the first avowedly anti-slavery candidate for the presidency of the United States.

John Forsythe, ex-governor of Georgia and secretary of state in President Martin Van Buren's cabinet, tried to stir up anti-Catholic sentiment in the South (and anti-Harrison sentiment at the same time) by linking the Catholic Church with the anti-southern abolitionists. But Bishop England was decidedly not an abolitionist, as he soon made crystal clear. Through a series of eighteen public letters, he traced the history and teachings of the Church on the slave question. He emphasized particularly that the Holy Father's encyclical condemned only the slave trade and not domestic slavery, a distinction also made by the United States government, whose laws forbade the slave traffic.

Writing to Forsythe, Bishop England recounted the various audiences he had had with Pope Gregory XVI concerning the subject of religion in Haiti. He said that he had pointed out to His Holiness that he was in a peculiar position, "that my being the bishop of a diocese, within the limits of which was contained the most numerous slave population in any diocese in the world, would render me unacceptable to the Haitian government, and that being engaged to transact the ecclesiastical organization of that island would probably render me unacceptable in my own diocese."

As already noted, Pope Gregory did not accept this objection, and Bishop England told Forsythe why:

> His Holiness met me by stating the very distinction to which I have been drawing your attention. "Though the south-

ern states of your union," said the Holy Father, "have had domestic slavery as an heirloom, whether they would or not, they are not engaged in the traffic — that is, the slave trade."

Thus, sir, I trust I have succeeded in showing that this letter of His Holiness which you described to be "an Apostolic Letter on Slavery" does, in fact, regard only that "slave trade" which the United States condemns, and not that domestic slavery which exists in our southern states.

This same emphasis had been made from the first time the pope's letter was printed in the *Miscellany* on March 14, 1840. With the pope's letter was printed Bishop England's interpretation in which he stated that the encyclical was directed against Spain and Portugal, whose "gross misconduct" in carrying on the slave traffic was "palpably cruel and demoralizing."

Bishop England went on to remind his readers that the United States government had condemned the slave traffic more than a quarter of a century previously and had armed its fleets for its suppression. He admitted that slavery itself still continued in the southern parts of the United States, but stated his belief that "it is impossible that it should be abolished for a considerable time to come without the most injurious results, not merely to property but also to society."

Bishop England believed that the physical conditions of the slaves in the South were equally as good as that of any laboring population in all of Christendom. He wrote that from his own experience, no truth seemed to him more evident than that the meddling of the northern abolitionists tended to retard the generous and humane efforts that the southern proprietors were making to increase the comforts and remedy the moral condition of the slaves. He wrote, "Whatever our wishes respecting slavery may be, we are firmly of the opinion that in all the South there is less cruelty and injustice committed against the slave by his owner than there is committed by the American abolitionists against the American slave owner."

That phrase "whatever our wishes respecting slavery may be" would seem to indicate that the bishop had some strong personal feelings about this subject. He did, and he expressed those feelings in a letter in the *Miscellany* dated February 25, 1841:

> I have been asked by many a question which I may as well answer at once — Whether I am friendly to the existence or continuation of slavery? I am not — but I also see the impossibility of now abolishing it here. When it can and ought to be abolished is a question for the legislature and not for me.

——•——

Bishop England apparently felt that his real mission in life was to ensure that his fellow Catholics were granted the religious freedom proclaimed in the Declaration of Independence and guaranteed in the Constitution. He believed profoundly in the democratic principles enunciated in those documents, and it was written of him that "he never apologized for his American citizenship nor bewailed the loss of anything worthwhile when he shook the dust of Europe from his heels." But ignorance, prejudice, and bigotry tried to deny Catholics their freedom.

One of the most viciously anti-Catholic publications of that era was the monthly magazine *The Theological Repertory*. In 1825, Bishop England wrote to the Rev. William Hawley, its publisher, and stated that he was at a total loss to understand why Hawley and other writers like him were so anxious and so unremitting in their attempts to interrupt the harmony that should exist between Catholics and Protestants in this country. He said, "In this happy country, Protestants and Catholics are united in bonds of amity; their intercourse is unrestrictedly affectionate," and that he could not understand why Hawley would want to "produce in America the miseries of European dissentions."

He asked:

Are these states become such a sink of ignorance that all the rejected falsehoods of Europe are to find an asylum here? Are we Americans, who have led the way in the career of a rational, well-regulated liberty, to crawl after the bigots of Europe, sucking in what they disgorge that we may vomit it upon each other? I protest. I cannot describe my feelings whilst I write; I thought I had flung the Atlantic between me and this necessity. I imagined that the testimony of George Washington would have had weight with the people of this Union. I did hope that the recollection of Archbishop Carroll was not altogether blotted out.

In 1826, Bishop England began a series of letters addressed to the Roman Catholics of the United States on the "Calumnies of J. Blanco White." White was an apostate priest whose anti-Catholic writings were widely circulated by Bishop Kemp, bishop of the Episcopal Church in Maryland, who used them as weapons to combat the progress of Catholics in the United States. Bishop England's letters exposed the psychology of Protestant prejudice toward the Catholic Church.

In his first letter, he wrote:

I am a native of Ireland, but a citizen of America, and, of course, have resided several years in this Union. I am a Roman Catholic. One of the principal inducements which operated on my mind in preferring this country to any other part of the world was not merely the excellence of its political institutions, but, as I flattered myself, the absence of bigotry ... I must confess that I have been somewhat disabused of my error.

He went on to say that he soon found that a Catholic, though legally and politically on a level with his fellow citizens, was too often looked upon as in some degree morally degraded. And this was, he said, mainly through ignorance of what the Church teaches.

To prove that the trouble was occasioned primarily through ignorance, Bishop England recounted his frequent opportunities to converse with polite and well-informed Protestant gentlemen. He said that these men would speak to him about the Catholic Church using the most offensive phraseology, absolutely unaware that the language they used was originally used to offend Catholics. Thus these men, quite innocently, would speak to the bishop about the Romish Church, and of Papish priests, or Romish bishops — all offensive terms. Or they would talk about Catholics adoring images, believing that Catholics actually did this.

England wrote that he knew these men meant well, and, though lamenting the mistake into which they had fallen in regard to the tenets and the general character of the Catholic religion, his respect for their kindness was increased. In fact, he wrote, "If our religion was what they were led to believe it was, very few, if any of us, would continue in communion with the Holy See."

For twenty-two years, from 1820 to 1842, John England was the outstanding spokesman for the Catholic Church in this country. For twenty-two years he had to defend the Church constantly against those who, either through ignorance or from malice, would try to deny Catholics their rights of religious freedom.

Time after time he denied the claim of Protestant leaders that the United States was a Protestant country. He ridiculed those who subscribed to the sentiments of the *Rochester Presbyterian Observer*, which openly declared, "There is no neutrality, no armistice, no yielding — onward — victory or death is the watchword of the Presbyterian Church. She will be the established church of the Union, or wade through blood to attain that just prerogative!"

He must have grown tired of continually reminding his opponents that the American Constitution allows freedom to all religions, but he was always quick to answer all charges made against the rights of the Church.

—•—

Bishop John England undoubtedly was one of the greatest orators this country has ever known. He was asked to speak wherever he traveled, whether in the United States, in Rome, or in other parts of Europe. Numerous descriptions of his power and eloquence have been written. A certain William George Reid of Baltimore, for example, wrote after one of England's sermons:

> Most of my readers have heard him preach and therefore can appreciate, as well as I, those exhibitions of stupendous power, so tempered with gentleness, that, while it struck objectors dumb, it never gave offense. If I were to attempt to describe the style of his controversial discourses, I would liken it to a straight bar of polished steel connecting his conclusion with his premises with the lightning of heaven blazing and flashing about it.

Brownson's Review, April 1850, said of his sermons: "The unlearned as well as the philosophical inquirer hung for hours on his lips whilst he discanted on the evidence of Christianity, and children fancied they understood what he propounded."

Bishop England would have had to have mastered the art of delivering a sermon, because most of his discourses were long and profound. The two-hour speech he gave before Congress was not unusual for him, and if his delivery was not perfected, his audiences would have grown fatigued. It was said that his gesticulations were sometimes almost too animated for the pulpit, but they were always perfectly in character, and they gave charm and effect to what he was saying. *Brownson's Review* gave this description of the bishop in the pulpit: "As he stood there, with folded arms, pausing at the close of some luminous argument and surveying his audience to discover whether they felt and acknowledged its force, all remained entranced. The effect of the oratorical pause was never seen to more advantage."

He always spoke without a manuscript, and his printed addresses are not faithful copies of the original addresses. They were usually written after the speech had been delivered, at the request of one who had heard the speech. One who heard Bishop England often said of the printed forms of his speeches, "They lack the spirit and all the other surroundings which gave life and vigor to the productions."

One of Bishop England's most powerful sermons was delivered in Boston on May 14, 1841. It was titled "On American Citizenship," and the occasion was prompted by the death of President William Henry Harrison only a month after he took his oath of office. President John Tyler proclaimed May 14 as a day of fast and prayer. Bishop England happened to be in Boston en route to Europe to beg funds for his impoverished diocese, and Boston's Bishop Benedict Fenwick prevailed upon him to give the sermon on that day. According to the *Boston Transcript* and the *Boston Pilot*, Bishop England outdid even himself that day. He spoke for two-and-a-half hours — "eloquently, brilliantly, powerfully, critically, and completely," said the *Transcript*, "and intensely imbued with the pure and holy spirit of heaven-borne charity and kindness."

The *Pilot* said:

> His irrefutable arguments and his exalted powers of reasoning may be reduced to paper. But the deep, impassioned earnestness, the majestic eloquence, the eye kindled with the fire of divine truth, the form rising with the lofty conceptions of the mind, the mute eloquence of the countenance, are characteristics of the sermon that none but those who were present can know.

It was in this speech that Bishop England developed his philosophy of democracy and emphasized that the Catholic Church was the pioneer in the republican form of government; indeed, she was the inspiration of the American experiment:

> Look through the records of the world, and see where the principles of true republicanism are first to be found. They had their origin in Christianity, and their earliest instance in the Church of which we are members. Her institutions are eminently republican. Her rulers are chosen by the common consent; her officers are obliged to account strictly to those over whom they preside; her guide is a written constitution of a higher force than the will of an individual. What call you this? Aristocracy? Monarchy? It is republicanism.

The conclusion he put forth from this was that Catholics can not only be good American citizens, but the best, because the freedoms of republicanism are familiar and natural to them.

—·—

One who knew him well had this final tribute to pay to Bishop John England:

> John England left behind him a name that will not be forgotten as long as virtue and piety and talents are respected and revered. As a Catholic, his faith was as strong as the rock of ages on which Christianity was founded; as a patriot, he had been trained in that school where the fiery ordeal of persecution was the test of his sincerity; as a scholar, his mind was profound, his imagination fertile and productive, his achievements various and extensive.
>
> As a citizen of the United States, there never breathed one more fervent in his admiration of the institutions he had sworn to protect, more religious in the observance of the duties which devolved upon him, and more devoted to the

country whose laws knew no distinction of classes, whose soil cherished and supported alike all sects of religion.

Never during his long and eventful career, whilst he defended his own religion, did he interfere with the religion of others. Those who knew him could not fail to feel towards him an almost filial affection. He was one of those great men who won the admiration of all. The goodness of his heart and the charm of his manners made warm friends of all who were fortunate enough to enjoy his acquaintance.

Archbishop John Hughes

The Catholics, whether of native or foreign birth, are willing to fight to the death for the support of the Constitution, the government, and the laws of the country.

— *ARCHBISHOP JOHN HUGHES*

CHAPTER 3

Archbishop John Hughes

O ne day in the 1860s, an American archbishop entered the royal chambers of Emperor Napoleon III of France. As he entered, the emperor bowed deeply while the empress, dressed simply and wearing no jewels, swept into a deep curtsy and then moved forward gracefully to genuflect and kiss the archbishop's ring.

The empress opened the conversation, asking about the archbishop's journey across the Atlantic Ocean. "Travelers say it is but a trifle now," she said.

"Imperial Lady, I am an old sailor," the archbishop answered. "And considering the December season the passage was pleasant but a little tedious. The ship took thirteen days instead of the eleven in ordinary times."

Emperor Napoleon asked about an old American friend. "Can you tell me, Monsignor, of General Winfield Scott? I knew him when I was in the United States."

Archbishop John Hughes of New York here saw an opportunity to emphasize his mission, for he had been sent by President Abraham Lincoln to France to present the cause of the North in a favorable light. The Civil War had begun in the United States, and it was known that England, because she needed cotton for her factory looms, was inclined to look favorably upon the South. It was very important to the North that France and the rest of Europe be kept neutral in the war. And, of all the people in the country, Archbishop

Hughes seemed the best possible choice as a spokesman for the Union.

But arranging for an audience with Napoleon III did not prove easy, even after the archbishop arrived on the continent. Many important officials feared that he spoke for the losing side and were none too cordial. So, John Hughes took matters into his own hands and wrote his own letter of introduction to the emperor, asking for an audience. A letter came back at once from the emperor and with it a gracious note from Empress Eugenie expressing pleasure at the prospect of receiving him at the Palace of the Tuileries.

So here he was, prepared to answer Napoleon's question about General Winfield Scott. He explained that, although Scott was a southerner, he had remained faithful to the Union. Indeed, he had been in command of the Union forces until a month before, when ill health had forced him to retire.

Turning aside to the empress, Archbishop Hughes told her that he had had the pleasure of baptizing the general's son. She was very interested and made a slight motion to one of her attendants, who quietly left the room.

Napoleon was primarily interested in knowing about the effectiveness of the blockade of the southern ports. He realized that the economy of the South depended on the sale of cotton and that the South probably would be unable to keep up the war if revenue from the sale of cotton were cut off. However, he had heard from his advisers that the blockade-runners were increasingly successful.

Archbishop Hughes had prepared himself well for his mission and was able to dispute the claims made by southern sympathizers among the emperor's advisers. He felt heartened that Napoleon listened to him carefully and nodded his head several times in apparent agreement.

As the audience was about to end, the empress's attendant returned to the room with the young prince imperial. Empress Eugenie took his hand and had the five-year-old boy make a formal bow to Archbishop Hughes and then asked the archbishop to give his blessing to their son. The boy knelt, and Archbishop Hughes gave him his blessing. Then he said:

> God bless you, my boy, and preserve you so that when you shall have grown up to be a man you may be able, under the divine benediction, to realize the good hopes that are entertained in your regard not only by your own country but by many other nations.

After meeting with Napoleon III and the Empress Eugenie, Archbishop Hughes went to Rome, where he had private talks with Pope Pius IX. The pope expressed his wish that a European nation or nations might be able to mediate the American Civil War and volunteered any help he could give to end the bloodshed.

President Lincoln and his secretary of state, William Seward, thought that Hughes' mission to France had been a success. The secretary gave a banquet in Washington in the archbishop's honor to give public, governmental recognition to his services, and Alexander Randall of Wisconsin, when he presented his credentials as American minister to the Papal States, spoke highly in praise of Hughes' efforts in aid of his country. He told Pope Pius that it was "a source of regret that the United States cannot in any appropriate way express its appreciation of such services." This seemed to be a delicate and diplomatic reference to President Lincoln's wish that Archbishop Hughes be considered for a cardinal's red hat.

But why was it felt that Archbishop Hughes would be the Union's best spokesman in Europe? It was simply because he had earned a reputation as a great patriot as well as a great archbishop. In his deep love for the United States, he believed that no issue, not even slavery, was great enough to imperil the unity of the nation. The thought of the secession of a state filled him with horror. He agreed wholeheartedly with Daniel Webster that liberty and union were one and inseparable. On August 23, 1861, he expressed his strong views on the subject this way:

I am an advocate of the sovereignty of every state in the Union within the limits recognized and approved of by its own representative authority when the Constitution was agreed upon ... But the Constitution having been formed by the common consent of all the parties engaged in the framework and approval thereof, I maintain that no state has a right to secede except in the manner provided in the document itself.

But, though he dreaded secession and detested slavery (in his youth he had written a poem, "The Slave," which was an outburst from his heart against slavery), he was opposed to the abolitionists whom he felt to be "radicals and heretics." Thus, he wrote to the secretary of war:

The Catholics ... whether of native or foreign birth, are willing to fight to the death for the support of the Constitution, the government, and the laws of the country. But if it should be understood ... that they are to fight for the abolition of slavery, then indeed they will turn away in disgust from the discharge of what would otherwise be a patriotic duty.

Hughes had been a staunch supporter of Lincoln, unlike most of the other Catholics of New York City, who were ardent supporters of Stephen A. Douglas. Perhaps Hughes' support of Lincoln stemmed in part from Hughes' friendship with Seward, but mainly Hughes could see the potential greatness in the tall, lanky gentleman from Illinois.

After the war began, Hughes was in frequent communication with Seward, and Seward showed many of the letters to President Lincoln. Lincoln at one time wrote to the archbishop to thank him for the "kind and judicious letters" he had written to Seward, "which he regularly allows me both the pleasure and profit of perusing." Lincoln particularly liked a letter in which Hughes counseled forbearance in victory and urged that the rebel leaders be treated in defeat with patience and consideration. "Conquest is not altogether by the sword," he had written. "Statesmanship may have much to do with it."

It was from these contacts with the administration that the idea was born to send Archbishop Hughes to Europe as an official ambassador of the United States. Hughes refused the ambassadorship, but gladly went to Europe in an unofficial capacity. Historians credit Hughes with success in preventing France from giving official recognition to the Confederacy even though sympathy in France was running high for the South. Many of the French thought that a separated South would be more sympathetic to France's ambitions in Mexico.

———•———

During the Civil War, the Catholics of the United States were as divided as the rest of the American citizens concerning secession and slavery. As to secession, Catholics in both the North and the South were fully in agreement that obedience to civil authority was a religious duty. However, the application of this principle was not easy during the war, for there was question of where the lawful authority rested. Catholics in the North held to the existing federal Union and hoped that the Union would be preserved. In the South, most of the bishops, priests, and their flocks considered secession an accomplished fact and therefore thought themselves obliged to transfer their loyalty to the Confederacy.

As to the issue of slavery, most Catholics in the North were opposed to slavery itself, but they were not abolitionists. Most Catholics in the South, on the other hand, felt that there was nothing morally wrong with slavery itself, only in the slave trade against which the pope had written. Or if they did consider slavery morally evil, as many of them did, they thought it would be much more unjust to some of the white men to have their property (the slaves) suddenly taken away from them. As we have seen, that was Bishop John England's position.

Catholics were active on both sides during the war. Archbishop Hughes wasn't the only Catholic bishop who worked for the governments of the North. Bishop Domenec of Pittsburgh was responsible for influencing Spain to remain neutral while Bishop Fitzpatrick of Boston exerted his influence with Belgium.

For the South, Bishop Patrick Lynch of Charleston was asked by Jefferson Davis to visit Europe on behalf of the Confederacy. Unfortunately for the South, however, his visit was ill-timed, because the fortunes of the South had already started to collapse. After the war, Bishop Lynch had difficulty getting permission to return to his diocese, but it was finally granted through the intercession of Archbishop Spalding of Baltimore, and with it came a pardon from President Andrew Johnson.

The bishops of both sides did all in their power to bring about a just and lasting peace. They were especially strengthened in their desires by special letters from the pope to Archbishop Hughes and Archbishop Odin of New Orleans in which he implored them to use their influence to bring the war to an end. They especially expressed their minds by the prayers and days of penance they prescribed in their dioceses.

Besides the Catholic prelates, the religious sisters made a profound impression on Catholics and non-Catholics alike during the war for their care of the wounded immediately behind the battle lines and in the hospitals. The nation's gratitude to these heroic nuns was expressed when the monument *Nuns of the Battlefield* was erected in Washington, D.C., to honor the more than six hundred sisters who did what they could to alleviate suffering, often at the risk of their own lives and in abominable sanitary conditions.

Many priests were also active participants in the war as chaplains. Forty priests served as chaplains in the northern army and twenty-eight in the southern army, although these figures are somewhat misleading because many of these priests served only a few months. In addition to those who served in the armies, President Lincoln appointed thirteen hospital chaplains.

One finds considerable similarity between Archbishop John Hughes of New York and Bishop John England of Charleston. Both were born in Ireland and, while being outspoken in their preference for the United States, retained a great affection for Ireland. Both spoke before a joint session of the United States Congress. Both were noted for their eloquent sermons. Both were known by their enemies as "Dagger John" because of their practice of signing their names with a cross in front of it, as do all Catholic bishops. And both were great patriots as well as courageous defenders of the Catholic Faith.

In addition to these similarities, Archbishop Hughes also had great reverence and admiration for Bishop England. He often quoted a statement on Americanism made by England in 1831. He knew it by heart, as did many of his priests from hearing it from him. Here is how the scene has been described:

> He would glare fiercely as he repeated the first words, for he wanted them taken as a statement of his own stand: "I am no renegade to Ireland; but I am now an American." The bishop would let that sink in; then he would continue to quote from Bishop England more calmly: "When, upon your approach to the polls, any person addresses you as an Irishman or a Frenchman or an Italian, or by any appellation but Carolinian or American, his language is distraint and offensive. He is either ignorant, or supposes you to be so, or has some other sinister view. There is a bribery of affections! There is a bribery in reminding you of the bravery and the patriotism and the generosity of the Irish. And all this is the more insulting as the object of the adulation, or the familiarity, is too plain to be mistaken. I warn you of your solemn serious obligation, that in giving your vote you recollect that you are an American!"

Hughes believed in this quotation to such an extent that at one point he objected to Secretary of State William Seward that it was improper to call the Sixty-ninth, Eighty-eighth and Sixty-third New York Regiments "the Irish Brigade." It wasn't that he didn't love Ireland, but he loved the United States more, because, as he said:

> In the annals of Church history there has never been a country which, in its civil and social relations, has exhibited so fair an opportunity for developing the practical harmonies of the Catholic Faith and Catholic charity as the United States.

John Hughes was born June 24, 1797, the third of seven children of Patrick and Margaret McKenna Hughes, in the village of Analoghan in County Tyrone, Ireland. This was then a land of Scottish "planters," and Catholics were bitterly persecuted. In 1816, Patrick Hughes, like so many other Irish Catholics, decided it was important for him to find a new life for his family in a country where there was no religious persecution. He and John's older brother, Patrick, sailed for America. John joined them a year later, traveling across the ocean alone.

After landing in the United States, John first found work as a gardener on Maryland's eastern shore. Later, he joined his father in Chambersburg, Pennsylvania. By 1818, the father and the two boys had saved enough money to bring John's mother and sisters to the United States, and the family was reunited.

Thirty miles from Chambersburg, in Emmitsburg, Maryland, Father John Dubois, who was later to become John Hughes' predecessor as Bishop of New York, had established Mount St. Mary's College, the first seminary for the training of priests in the United States. John had always wanted to be a priest, a desire his mother encouraged to the fullest extent. At her suggestion, he applied for and received the job of gardener at the seminary with the hope that he might eventually be able to study for the priesthood.

John had great talent as a gardener, but Father Dubois was more impressed by the way the young man would seize any opportunity to study. He finally allowed John to enter the seminary as a student. John was ordained on October 15, 1826, in St. Joseph's Church, Philadelphia, and was soon assigned to this same church as pastor.

The people of this Quaker city found Father Hughes to be the most vigorous pastor Philadelphia had ever known. (This was before St. John Neumann was bishop of Philadelphia.) He was determined that his parishioners would be good Catholics — and good citizens. And he was determined, too, to fight for the rights of the Catholics of Philadelphia to make sure they would enjoy the freedom of religion guaranteed them by the Constitution — for he remembered how he and his family had been denied that freedom in Ireland.

Father Hughes first attracted national attention on May 31, 1829, when he delivered a stirring sermon prompted by the signing, by King George IV of England, of a bill emancipating English Catholics from the laws that discriminated against them. Great celebrations were planned in the United States, and in Philadelphia these celebrations were climaxed by a Mass in Old St. Augustine's Church. Father Hughes was selected to preach the sermon since it was well-known that he was deeply affected by the signing of the Catholic Emancipation Bill because he had known personal sufferings in his boyhood from the restrictions that were now removed.

The church was filled, and the crowd spilled out into the streets as Father Hughes ascended the pulpit. With a voice that was described as "clear, sonorous, and tenderly sympathetic," he stirred the people's hearts. An account of the sermon reported:

> Those standing at the crowded back of the church kept
> shouting behind them to the people in the streets the stirring
> phrases of the great sermon. The people closest re-echoed
> them and passed them on. It was odd in the silence of the

church to hear cheers outside as a telling bit of eloquent speech found kinship in the people's hearts.

The sermon was later published in pamphlet form, and it immediately made Father John Hughes an important national Catholic figure.

In 1830, Bishop Francis Patrick Kenrick succeeded Bishop Conwell as bishop of Philadelphia, and Father Hughes became his secretary and right-hand man. During this time, Father Hughes established a diocesan newspaper, *The Catholic Herald*, and became its editor.

Then Father Hughes was again thrust into national prominence. This time he was challenged to a written debate by the Rev. John Breckinridge, one of the most noted Protestant clergymen of the day. For several months the debate raged through the secular journals in Philadelphia. When it was over it was generally thought that the Catholic priest had won the better of it.

Breckinridge wasn't heard of again for four years. Then he resurfaced with a second challenge for debate; it was on the question: "Is the Roman Catholic religion, in any and all of its principles and doctrines, inimical to civil or religious liberty?"

During this debate, Hughes wrote about the teachings of the Jesuit cardinal and saint, Robert Bellarmine, whose ideas and writings are so woven into the American Constitution. He wrote about both Charles Carroll of Carrollton, who died only two years previously, and Archbishop John Carroll, who was widely known as an outstanding patriot. And he wrote about the many times President George Washington had expressed his appreciation to the Catholics for their aid in the cause of liberty.

By coincidence, John Hughes became bishop of New York the same year Bishop England died in Charleston — 1842. Hughes had been consecrated as coadjutor bishop of New York with right of succession on January 7, 1838, and was full administrator of the diocese within two weeks because two successive paralytic attacks had made Bishop John Dubois an invalid. Bishop Dubois died on December 20, 1842. He was then forty-five years old.

———•———

The year 1844 saw the rise of the so-called Native American political party (the "Nativists"). This party, bitterly anti-Catholic, had provoked riots in Philadelphia, where two churches and rectories and two convents had been burned, forty people had been killed, more than sixty had been seriously injured, and eighty-one homes had been looted or destroyed. When this happened, Philadelphia's Bishop Kenrick asked his flock to bear with the outrages, to return good for evil, to do nothing to fight back. "Rather let every church burn than shed one drop of blood or imperil one precious soul," he said.

This may have been all right for Bishop Kenrick and the Catholics of Philadelphia, but Bishop Hughes wasn't made that way. He believed in standing up for his and his flock's rights. "If any single Catholic church is burned in New York," he warned, "the city will become a second Moscow." The reference was to the burning of the Russian city by Napoleon Bonaparte's soldiers.

On election day of 1844, a mob of twelve hundred Nativists paraded through New York's streets, shouting insults at the Irish Catholics. This was the way the Philadelphia riots had begun. The mob swung into Spring Street toward the old St. Patrick's Cathedral on Mott Street. "But there they halted," said Bishop Hughes later, "for a reason they had." Two thousand well-armed members of the Ancient Order of Hibernians were waiting for them. The Nativists were at least smart enough to disperse.

A few weeks later, a Nativist mass meeting was planned for City Hall Park — to be addressed by the leaders of the Philadelphia rioters. Bishop Hughes organized men to guard every Catholic church in New York, and then he personally strode down to City Hall to see the mayor, Robert H. Morris. "I did not come to tell you what to do," he told the mayor. "I am a churchman, not the mayor of New

York. But if I were the mayor, I would examine the laws of the state and see if there were not attached to the police force a battery of artillery and a company or so of artillery, and a squadron of horse. I think I should find that there were; and if so — *I should call them out!*" The mass meeting was canceled.

—·—

In 1845, when war with Mexico seemed close at hand, Secretary of State James Buchanan, at President James Polk's suggestion, asked Bishop Hughes if he would go to Mexico to try to settle the rival claims of the two countries to California and Texas without bloodshed. Unfortunately, however, Buchanan's request came too late. Before Hughes could reply to the request, Mexican troops crossed the border into Texas, and the war began. It was too late for the bishop to go to Mexico.

During the Mexican War, John Hughes took an active interest in the spiritual welfare of the Catholics in the army — and there were quite a few, too. The *Freeman's Journal* reported, "It must be a source of pride to the Irish Catholic citizens to know that General (Zachary) Taylor's army consists of more than one-half of their countrymen." A total of 3,676 Irish-born men enlisted during the two years of the war, and, through John Hughes' urging, President Polk appointed two Jesuit priests as chaplains to them. These were the first Catholic priests to serve with the armed forces of the United States.

By this time, the ruling statesmen of the nation recognized Bishop Hughes as the leading voice of Catholics in the United States. So, in 1847 he was invited to speak before a joint session of Congress. The chamber of the House of Representatives and the visitors' galleries were packed as he ascended the rostrum. With his usual eloquence, he spoke on the subject "Christianity — the Only Source of Moral, Social, and Political Regeneration." At the close of the speech it was reported that he was "greeted with a tumult of applause." One of those who listened carefully to him was a tall, gaunt congressman from the state of Illinois, Abraham Lincoln.

In 1850, Pope Pius IX made New York an archdiocese, and John Hughes became the first archbishop of New York. The dioceses of Albany, Buffalo, Boston, and Hartford were placed under his jurisdiction.

One of his dreams as archbishop of New York was to build a magnificent cathedral to take the place of the one on Mott Street. The cathedral would be Gothic, and he wanted James Renwick Jr. to be his architect. Finally, he found the site for his cathedral, far out from what was then the city, for Archbishop Hughes had great visions of how the city of New York would grow:

> The city is built on an island. The movement of its growth must always be northward. I see it going past my own house, creeping up on it and going past, far out as that dwelling is. I can see the city sweeping past this once outlying village of Elgin up to Yorkville and Harlem, to Bloomingdale and Riverdale, taking to itself all the little villages ... The middle road is broad. A cathedral facing on it will have a commanding prospect. I am firm in my conviction that in time to come this will be the heart of the city. And my cathedral, God's cathedral, will be a heart of pulsating prayer at the city's center.

From 1853 to 1858, James Renwick worked on the plans for the vast building. Archbishop Hughes worked with him, determined to have nothing but the best because he was building for the generations to come. The contract for the building of the cathedral was finally let for a cost of 867,500 dollars, and a ceremony for the laying of the cornerstone was scheduled for the feast of the Assumption in the year 1858.

The crowds that assembled for the laying of the cornerstone were beyond anyone's wildest estimates. *The New York Times* stated that on that August day the city was deserted because everyone was at the cathedral site. The *Times* estimated some hundred thousand people present, either "floating or persistently present."

Work on the building went slowly and was finally interrupted completely by the Civil War. When the war broke out, Archbishop Hughes, in his intense patriotism, had the Stars and Stripes flown from the scaffolding of the new cathedral as well as over the old St. Patrick's. And when he was attacked for thus seemingly linking Church and State, Hughes answered:

> I am getting old, and I know this world would have gone on as well as it has if I had never lived. But I have not been able to sever my feelings and thoughts from this the only country I call mine and to which I am devoted by every prompting of my understanding and every loyal sentiment of my heart.

—·—

Strange as it would seem, especially since Archbishop Hughes had been in the service of, and honored by, the Republican government in power during the Civil War, he and all Catholics became the target of the fanatically abolitionist Republican press in the city of New York. Although the archbishop himself probably tended to be a Republican, most Catholics in New York were Democrats, and the Democratic Party was considered pro-slavery. Horace Greeley in the *Tribune* and William Cullen Bryant in the *Post* attacked the Catholics because they separated the preservation of the Union from the freeing of the slaves.

Then came the draft law — a law that was denounced as unconstitutional by both the governor of New York, Horatio Seymour, and the mayor of New York City, Fernando Wood. Some of the provisions of the law were unfair; for example, a man could buy himself a substitute for three hundred dollars and free himself of the obligation to serve in the army. The common citizens of New York claimed this provision penalized the poor since they couldn't raise such a sum.

Horace Greeley and William Cullen Bryant, however, were heartily in favor of the law, and as opposition to it grew, Greeley accused Archbishop Hughes of being responsible for the opposition. Actually, the archbishop was in favor of a draft if it would bring the war to a quicker end, although he was not in favor of exempting the rich from their obligation to serve their country. He had even gone so far as to order his name removed from the masthead of the *Metropolitan Record*, his unofficial organ, when the editor advocated open resistance to the draft.

Opposition to the draft law grew ever stronger until, on July 11, 1863, rioting began. For four days New York was the scene of death and destruction, particularly against black people. For the poor workers of the city not only resented the law which discriminated against the poor, but also the government's policy of bringing black slaves in from the South. The workers, a great many of whom were Irish, claimed that these southern blacks were willing to work for less money and were taking away many of the unskilled jobs available in New York. They were also angered because black people were exempt from the draft law. A man summed up the anger against the blacks this way: "They were not being forced to help free their fellows; yet white men, family men, were being asked to let their children starve while exempt Negroes took their jobs."

At this time, Archbishop Hughes was suffering from crippling rheumatism and the kidney ailment that was soon to kill him. So, he was unable to go out into the city. His priests, however, were able to report to him that Catholics were not responsible for the riots, as had been claimed by Greeley and Bryant. On the contrary, the riots were being led by anti-Catholic and anti-black elements. Indeed, Catholics had been in the forefront of attempts to stop the rioting.

Upon learning this, Hughes immediately wrote to Horace Greeley, but Greeley waited until the second day of the rioting to publish the letter. Hughes wrote:

In spite of Mr. Greeley's assault on the Irish, in the present disturbed condition of the city I will appeal not only to them but to all persons who love God and revere the holy Catholic religion which they profess to return to their homes with as little delay as possible.

When the rioting continued, Archbishop Hughes issued a call to his people to assemble before his Madison Avenue residence. The call, addressed to "the men of New York who are now called in many of the papers rioters," explained that the archbishop was not able, because of his rheumatism, to visit them. But he said that there was no reason why they should not pay him a visit, "in your whole strength." He asked them, then, to come to his residence on Friday at two o'clock and he would have a speech prepared for them. "If I am unable to stand during its delivery," he said, "you will permit me to address you sitting. My voice is much stronger than my limbs."

William Cullen Bryant, in the *Post*, called this plea a shepherd's summoning of "the wolves ... miscreant, assassins, robbers, house-burners, and thieves, such a congregation of vicious and abandoned wretches as is not often got together." He urged any "sheep" among the Catholics to stay away. But they did not stay away. They responded in a great mass of men that extended up and down Madison Avenue. Many of them were the same ones who had defended the cathedral and other churches against the Nativist attacks in 1844.

Archbishop Hughes was helped to a chair on the balcony. He gazed over the quiet throng and then began to speak:

Men of New York! They call you rioters, but I cannot see a rioter's face among you ... If I could have met you anywhere else but here I would have gone, even on crutches. For I address you as your father ... If you are Irishmen as your enemies say you are, I am an Irishman, too — and I am not a rioter. No, I am a man of peace. If you are Catholics, I am Catholic, too ...

If property is destroyed, it can be replaced; but if lives are lost, the departed souls cannot be recalled from the other world ... I counsel you not to give up your principles and convictions; but keep out of the crowds in which immortal souls are launched into eternity without a moment's notice ...

Never mind these reports, these calumnies, as I hope they are, against you and against me, that you are rioters and this and that. Go now to your homes with my blessing. And if you by chance, as you disperse, should meet a military man or a policeman, just *look* at him.

He then got up painfully and was helped off the balcony. There was quiet and then thunderous cheering until he reappeared at the window and waved gently. Then the men quietly went home.

———

This was the last time most of those men were to see their beloved archbishop, for John Hughes was sicker than realized. Indeed, he had already said his last Mass a full two months before the draft riots and his speech. He died shortly after 7:30 p.m. on January 3, 1864, at the age of sixty-seven.

All flags in the city were at half-staff during the funeral and all city offices were closed for the day, because, as Mayor G. Godfrey Gunther wrote:

It is not that an eloquent and exalted prelate has passed away — but that in his death our country has lost an eminent citizen and pure patriot; for this we may mingle our tears with those of others bound by the most sacred ties to the departed.

From Washington, Secretary Seward wrote on behalf of President Lincoln to express the "sorrow with which he received intelligence of that distinguished prelate's demise." He recalled that Archbishop Hughes "did the nation a service with all the loyalty, fidelity, and practical wisdom which, on so many other occasions, illustrated his great ability for administration."

And on his own behalf, Seward wrote of "the respect and affection which I have so long cherished towards him as a faithful friend, a pious prelate, a loyal patriot, a great and good man."

Cardinal James Gibbons

You were pleased to mention my pride in being an American citizen. It is the proudest earthly title I possess.

— *CARDINAL JAMES GIBBONS*

CHAPTER 4

—•◦•╍•◦•—

Cardinal James Gibbons

On the feast of St. Patrick in the year 1887, James Gibbons knelt in the Vatican Hall of the Consistory to receive from Pope Leo XIII the giant-brimmed, gold-tasseled galero, the red hat that is the symbol of the office of cardinal in the Catholic Church. Gibbons became the second cardinal in the history of the Catholic Church in the United States.

Eight days later, Cardinal Gibbons took formal possession of his titular or parish church in Rome, the Basilica of Santa Maria in Trastevere. (Every cardinal is assigned as pastor of a church in Rome.) This occasion was the first opportunity he had to make a public statement as a cardinal, and Gibbons had decided that this statement would be a strong defense of the separation of Church and State as it existed in the United States.

So, on March 25, the young cardinal ascended the pulpit of a church filled to capacity with the most important officials of the Catholic Church and began his sermon. An eyewitness account reported, "There was at first a faint tremor, and his voice quavered as he began, but it soon gathered strength and firmness, until every word he uttered could be heard distinctly throughout the vast edifice."

The new cardinal quickly reviewed the history of the Catholic Church in America, pointing out that "where only one bishop was found in the beginning of this century, there are now seventy-five exercising spiritual jurisdiction." Then he electrified his audience with his next statement: "For this great progress we are indebted under God and the fostering vigilance of the Holy See *to the civil liberty we enjoy in our enlightened republic.*"

He did not stop there. Alluding to Pope Leo XIII's recent encyclical *Immortale Dei*, in which the Holy Father had stated that the Church is not committed to any form of government but adapts to all, Cardinal Gibbons declared that the Church had often been hampered and even forced to struggle for her existence when "despotism has cast its dark shadow." But, he said, "in the general atmosphere of liberty she blossoms like a rose." He continued:

> For myself, as a citizen of the United States, without closing my eyes to our defects as a nation, I proclaim, with a deep sense of pride and gratitude, and in this great capital of Christendom, that I belong to a country where the civil government holds over us the aegis of its protection without interfering in the legitimate exercise of our sublime mission as ministers of the Gospel of Jesus Christ.
>
> Our country has liberty without license, authority without despotism. Hers is no spirit of exclusiveness. She has no frowning fortifications to repel the invader, for we are at peace with all the world. In the consciousness of her strength and of her good will to all nations she rests secure. Her harbors are open in the Atlantic and Pacific to welcome the honest immigrant who comes to advance his temporal interest and to find a peaceful home.
>
> But while we are acknowledged to have a free government, we do not perhaps receive due credit for possessing also a strong government. Yes, our nation is strong, and her strength lies, under Providence, in the majesty and supremacy of the law, in the loyalty of her citizens to that law, and in the affection of our people for their free institutions.

It took courage for Cardinal Gibbons to make that statement, because, at that time in history, Rome was distrustful of the separation of Church and State. The union of Church and State had begun centuries before when every ruler was also a Catholic subject and union was natural. Under this union, the Church had gained ascendancy, primarily because of the theologians' formula of the primacy of the soul over the body. However, in recent years in Europe, Church and State were in conflict more than in harmony. During Pope Pius IX's reign, the Church had lost the Papal States, and both Pope Pius and Pope Leo XIII were self-imposed prisoners in the Vatican. In France, Italy, and Germany, hostile governments interfered with the Church and in some cases actively persecuted it.

Thus, Cardinal Gibbons believed ardently in the advisability of the separation of Church and State as it existed in the United States. Both as the patriot he was and as a churchman, he rejoiced in the First Amendment to the Constitution that assured no government interference with Church affairs. "A Catholic finds himself at home in the United States," he once said. "Nowhere else can he breathe more freely that atmosphere of divine truth which alone can make him free."

In 1884, after a trip to Europe, he observed, "The oftener I go to Europe, the longer I remain there, and the more I study the political situation of the people, the more profoundly grateful I am to be an American citizen."

Cardinal Gibbons spoke his mind about this issue many times, but the way he liked to express himself best was with a story about an old Scotsman who gravely told a friend, "Sandy, Sandy, honesty is the best policy. I know because I've tried both." Then the cardinal would say, "The Church has tried both union of Church and State and independent operation. For my part, I would be sorry to see the relations of the Church and the State any closer than they are at present."

But the cardinal's speech in Rome on March 25, 1887, was the first time he or anyone else had spoken thus to the Catholic Church officials in the Vatican. As might be expected, there was immediate reaction. The European Catholic press criticized the sermon, but the American press was unanimous in its praise. The *Baltimore Sun* exclaimed, "Those who heard it pronounced the address magnificent!" The *New York Herald* ran the entire text together with an editorial praising the speech. The Baltimore *Catholic Mirror* asserted that "no such words have been uttered by an American bishop since Archbishop Carroll founded the see of Baltimore."

The cardinal's speech had its effect upon the pope, too. A year later, when Pope Leo was celebrating his golden jubilee as a priest, United States President Grover Cleveland, after consulting with Cardinal Gibbons, sent as a gift an elaborate vellum copy of the United States Constitution, hand-lettered in Old English and elegantly bound in red and white. Upon receiving it, the frail old pontiff said:

> You enjoy in America perfect freedom. That freedom, we admit, is highly beneficial to the spread of religion. Toward America I bear a special love. Your government is free, your future full of hope. Your president commands my highest admiration.

Later, Cardinal Gibbons received a letter from Pope Leo expressing admiration for the Constitution of the United States, "not only because it enables industrious and enterprising citizens to attain so high a degree of prosperity, but also because under its protection your Catholic countrymen have enjoyed a liberty which has so confessedly promoted the astonishing growth of their religion in the past, and will, we trust, enable it in the future to be of the highest advantage to the civil order as well."

Cardinal Gibbons showed this letter to President Grover Cleveland, who asked to be permitted to keep it, a request promptly granted.

The period in United States history from the Civil War through World War I (approximately 1860 to 1920) covers a lot of territory

— both literally and figuratively. This was the time when the United States grew the most, populating the states in the West. This was also the time of greatest growth of the Catholic Church in America, both in numbers and in influence.

Beyond a doubt, the person who most dominated this period of United States history, so far as the Catholic Church is concerned, was Cardinal James Gibbons. He was a young priest during the Civil War and an adviser to President Wilson in 1920 (although he was not as good of a friend of Wilson's as he was of some of Wilson's predecessors).

Just as the nation could be described as in its adolescent years following the Civil War, so the Church was in its turbulent years, struggling through persecution to become the powerful mature body it was by 1921, the year of Cardinal Gibbons' death. And it was no easy struggle, for the Church had to fight its growing pains just as the nation did.

First, the Church in America had to make itself understood by Church officials in the Vatican, to whom America was still considered a vast mission territory. Indeed, in 1875, when Pope Pius IX created America's first cardinal in the person of John McCloskey of New York, the papal secretary of state, Cardinal Antonelli, is said to have exclaimed, "But His Holiness must be mad!" And the idea of the separation of Church and State, which Cardinal Gibbons tried to explain in his speech after being made a cardinal, found only distrust in Rome. Church officials were unable to comprehend such an idea since history had shown that if the Church and State were not united in friendship, the State would persecute the Church.

Just as the American idea had to be explained to Rome, so too did the Catholic Church have to be explained to America. To "native Americans," the vast horde of immigrants, first from Ireland and later from southern Europe, seemed like an invasion, and, as their forefathers had done, they were prepared to fight for their land.

As if these difficulties weren't enough, the Church in America also had ecclesiastical problems within itself. Bitter arguments between strong-willed prelates were to try the patience of the new cardinal from Baltimore, particularly over the "Americanization" of the Church. Liberal bishops, headed by Archbishop John Ireland of St. Paul, Minnesota, and conservative bishops, headed by Archbishop Michael Corrigan of New York, were to make headlines throughout the country and, eventually, lead to the "phantom heresy" of Americanism. (This is covered more thoroughly in the chapter about Father Isaac Hecker.)

As industrialization came to America, along with it came labor problems. The Church was once again in the middle, and once again it was up to Cardinal Gibbons to lead the way.

This "era of Cardinal Gibbons" was certainly not a peaceful time for the leaders of the Church in America. But growth is never easy to manage. The character of the Church in the United States today was molded during that period, and it is fortunate, both for the country and the Church, that courageous patriots were at the helm of the spiritual ship in America.

During Cardinal Gibbons' life he was widely known as an extraordinary patriot and beloved citizen. In 1916, when the cardinal was 82, former President Theodore Roosevelt said to him: "Taking your life as a whole, I think that you now occupy the position of being the most respected and venerated and useful citizen of our country," a most extraordinary statement for any president to make to anyone.

The most impressive ceremony in honor of Cardinal Gibbons undoubtedly was the celebration of his twenty-fifth anniversary as a cardinal and his fiftieth anniversary as a priest on June 6, 1911. This public demonstration by the nation's leaders was a purely civic and non-sectarian affair in honor of James Gibbons as a private citizen. President William Howard Taft was present and gave the principal address, the first of ten such addresses. The president said:

> What we are especially delighted to see confirmed in him and his life is the entire consistency which he has demon-

strated between earnest and single-minded patriotism and love of country on the one hand and sincere devotion to his Church on the other. Notwithstanding the often delicate and complicated nature of the questions proposed to him, he rarely if ever made a mistake.

Following President Taft was former President Theodore Roosevelt, who stated:

No church in the United States will ever have to defend itself as long as those standing highest in that church serve the people, devoting their lives to the service of men and women around them, as you, Cardinal Gibbons, have devoted your life to the service of your fellow countrymen.

Senator Elihu Root stressed the cardinal's insistence on the separation of Church and State and pointed out that "our American doctrine of separation of Church and State does not involve the separation of the people of America from religious belief."

Others honoring Cardinal Gibbons included Chief Justice Edward White, Speaker of the House of Representatives Bennett Champ Clark, and many other government officials — so many, in fact, that the *Washington Post* reported, "The business of the United States government, superficially at least, was at a standstill yesterday, owing to the exodus of public men to attend the anniversary ceremonies." Reporting on the ceremonies the next day, the same paper said, "Such a demonstration was never before seen on this hemisphere."

When it was Cardinal Gibbons' chance to reply, he said to President Taft, "You were pleased to mention my pride in being an American citizen. It is the proudest earthly title I possess."

———

It takes quite a man to earn eulogies such as these, and Cardinal James Gibbons was quite a man. The fourth child and first son of

Thomas and Bridget Walsh Gibbons, he was born on July 23, 1834, in Baltimore. Three years later, Thomas Gibbons fell ill and, under doctors' advice, took his family to Ireland for a visit because it was felt that the climate there would be better for his health. The visit turned out to be for sixteen years, six years after Thomas's death. Finally, in 1853, Bridget Gibbons brought her family back to the United States and settled in New Orleans. James was then nineteen.

James was always a religious youth, and one day he heard that Father Isaac Hecker and some other Redemptorists were giving a mission at St. Joseph's Church in New Orleans. He attended the mission, and before it was over decided that he had a vocation to the priesthood. In September of 1855, at age twenty-one, he entered St. Charles College at Ellicott City, just outside Baltimore.

He later advanced to St. Mary's Seminary in Baltimore for philosophy and theology courses and graduated at the top of his class. He was ordained on June 30, 1861, and was assigned as curate of St. Patrick's Church, near Fell's Point in Baltimore.

The Civil War had already begun and Father Gibbons had to make a difficult decision. Although his heart was on the side of the South (his family still lived in New Orleans, and his brother was an officer in the Confederate Army), his convictions were with the Union. He took on duties as chaplain to soldiers at Fort Marshall and Fort McHenry. One day a Confederate soldier was captured while visiting his family. He was sentenced to hang. Gibbons argued that the boy was not a spy and had not been a combatant at the time of his arrest; thus he should not be hanged. He felt so strongly about the matter that he wrote to President Lincoln asking for a reprieve for the boy. The reprieve arrived the night the soldier was to be executed.

After the war was over, the soldier came to see Father Gibbons. "Since you did not have the opportunity to tie the knot around my neck before, I ask you now to tie a happier one," he said, and he asked the priest to officiate at his wedding.

Three days after the Battle of Gettysburg, Archbishop Francis P. Kenrick of Baltimore died, and in July of 1864, Martin J. Spalding was named the new archbishop. Spalding had heard nothing but excellent reports about Father Gibbons and soon asked him to serve as his episcopal secretary.

In 1866, Archbishop Spalding called a plenary council of bishops to Baltimore and trusted Father Gibbons to plan and run the council. One problem discussed at the council was the need for more bishops. The council drew up a *terna*, a list of three candidates, for each area in need of a bishop, and Father Gibbons found himself in first place on the lists for Erie, Pennsylvania, and for the state of North Carolina. Two years later, he was appointed bishop of North Carolina — the youngest bishop in the world at the age of thirty-four.

North Carolina was by no means an ecclesiastical prize. In the entire state of nearly fifty thousand square miles there were only "about seven hundred" Catholics out of a population of a million. Bishop Gibbons had only three priests to help him. After enthroning him in Wilmington, Archbishop Spalding returned to Baltimore and wrote to the new bishop: "I was truly affected when I left you Monday morning. I thought you looked like an orphan."

A year after being consecrated bishop, Gibbons joined the other Catholic prelates in Rome for the First Vatican Council, at which the doctrine of papal infallibility was proclaimed and defined. "An ecumenical council is probably the greatest sight on earth!" he exclaimed when he saw the magnificence of Rome after working in the primitive conditions of his diocese.

As the youngest bishop present, he decided to talk little and listen much because he wanted to take advantage of the opportunity to learn from Church officials from throughout the world. "So keen was my appreciation at being present among these venerable men," he wrote, "that I cannot remember to have missed a single session, and I was a most attentive listener at all the debates."

Back in the United States after the council, John McGill, the bishop of Richmond, died, and the pope appointed Gibbons bishop of Richmond in addition to his duties as bishop of North Carolina. Then Archbishop Spalding died, and Bishop James Roosevelt Bayley of Newark, New Jersey, was appointed to succeed him. Archbishop Bayley was already an old man and ill much of the time, so he persuaded Bishop Gibbons to make frequent trips from Richmond to Baltimore to help with administering the Archdiocese of Baltimore.

In 1877, Archbishop Bayley asked Bishop Gibbons if he would consent to become his coadjutor with the right of succession. Gibbons said he would if the other archbishops of the United States would indicate their approval in writing to Rome. The other archbishops did approve, and Bayley sent to Rome the required list of three names with Gibbons in first place.

Rome duly appointed Gibbons to the post, but before the transfer could take place, Archbishop Bayley died, and Gibbons thus became archbishop of Baltimore at the age of forty-three — the youngest archbishop in the world, just as he earlier had been the youngest bishop. He was named a cardinal ten years later, in 1887.

———

Archbishop Gibbons was a champion of the laboring man. This was a period of history when this role required more than ordinary courage. Gibbons displayed this courage, even to the extent of arguing with some of the most powerful officials in the Vatican.

The life of a laborer at the end of the nineteenth century was completely different from the life of a laborer today. In those days, plant managers and industrialists held the upper hand, and, in many cases, the workers were little more than slaves. In fact, Cardinal William O'Connell of Boston, in 1916, recalling his own youth as a worker in a textile mill, remarked, "An ordinary slave in the South, under a humane master, was leading a far more human existence."

To combat these conditions, Uriah S. Stephens, a Mason and an Odd Fellow, founded the Noble and Holy Order of the Knights of Labor in 1869. By necessity, this organization was a secret society because employers would immediately fire any employees who they discovered belonged to the society. From Stephens' association with the Masonic Order came the Knights of Labor's secret password, handgrip, and other trappings of secret societies.

While the need for secrecy was clear to the laboring man, it was not so clear to Church officials, who considered the Knights of Labor similar to the Masons, which had been condemned by Rome a century earlier. Thus, some prelates forbade Catholics under their jurisdiction to join the Knights. Archbishop Bayley, for example, stated: "These miserable associations called labor organizations are subversive of government and communistic. No Catholic with any idea of the spirit of his religion will encourage them."

In Canada, Archbishop Elzear A. Taschereau of Quebec queried Rome about these labor organizations, forwarding a copy of the constitution of the Knights of Labor. In 1884 the answer arrived: "These societies ought to be considered among those prohibited." Archbishop Taschereau then announced that any of his subjects who persisted in being members of the Knights of Labor would be excommunicated from the Church.

This did not settle the matter for the United States, however, and opinion was strongly divided among the bishops, with Archbishop John Ireland of St. Paul championing the Knights and Archbishop Michael Corrigan of New York leading those who believed that "the Knights are undoubtedly forbidden."

At this point Archbishop Gibbons displayed one of his outstanding attributes — his prudence. Rather than do something hurriedly, he wanted to learn all he could about the problem. "A masterly inactivity and a vigilant eye on the proceedings is perhaps the best thing to be done in the present juncture," he counseled. First, he visited President Grover Cleveland to get his views on the matter and learned that the president saw no threat to the government from the Knights of Labor and that he saw justice in many of their claims.

Gibbons then called in Terence V. Powderly, the grand master workman of the Knights and a Catholic, and questioned him about the organization. Gibbons told Powderly frankly that he believed in labor's right to organize and he approved of strikes when absolutely necessary to obtain the just rights of the laboring man. However, he said, he disliked the idea of a closed shop because each worker should have the right to his own decision regarding union membership and should not be denied the right to work if he chose to remain non-union. Powderly then assured Gibbons that there was nothing contrary to the Catholic Church in the Knights of Labor and that the need for secrecy was gradually evaporating.

Gibbons then invited Powderly to present his case to a meeting of the country's archbishops. Powderly did so, and a long discussion of the Knights of Labor took place. Gibbons told the other archbishops, "I would regard the condemnation of the Knights of Labor as disastrous to the Church." When a vote took place, however, two of the twelve archbishops voted for condemnation, and only a unanimous vote could settle the issue.

Gibbons therefore decided to take the matter directly to the Congregation of the Holy Office in Rome — a bold step, but one Gibbons considered extremely important for the Church in the United States. Gibbons could foresee that if the Knights of Labor were condemned, the Church could lose thousands of Catholic workers. Furthermore, he felt that his native America, which he loved enough to risk ecclesiastical disapproval, would regard the ban as foreign meddling in American affairs.

Early in 1887, when he went to Rome to receive his red hat designating him as a cardinal, Gibbons called in person on every member of the Congregation of the Holy Office in an attempt to change their earlier ban. Finally, after what Gibbons' first biographer, Allen Sinclair Will, called a "heated interview in which he declared that he would hold the Commissary of the Holy Office, Vincenza Sallua, personally responsible for the loss of souls in the United States if the organization was condemned," he won a promise of reconsideration.

Then Gibbons, with the help of Archbishop John Ireland and Bishop John Keane, both of whom had been in Rome for some time trying to prepare the way for the cardinal, put his plea in writing. He sent to Cardinal Giovanni Simeoni, the Prefect of the Propaganda, his famous memorial on the Knights of Labor. This memorial has been described, depending on the describer's point of view, as "one of the great charters of the labor movement" and "a shrewd mixture of moral principle and expediency."

The memorial began by explaining that the Knights of Labor should not be condemned because it was not a secret organization with oaths of blind obedience. The cardinal cited President Cleveland as authority for denying that the organization was unpatriotic, adding, "The United States Congress is at present engaged in framing measures for the improvement of the condition of the laboring class." He defended the working man's right to protect himself by organizing as "a means altogether natural and just."

The memorial also touched upon the problem mentioned above of the Church meddling in American affairs. Gibbons told Cardinal Simeoni that both political parties in the United States were proclaiming the rights of the workers and that it would be "no less ridiculous than rash" to "crush by an ecclesiastical condemnation an organization which represents more than five hundred thousand votes and which has already so respectably and so universally recognized a place in the political arena." He pointed out that "the accusation of being un-American — that is to say, alien to our national spirit — is one of the most powerful weapons which the enemies of the Church can employ against her." Finally, the cardinal said that Catholic workers "love the Church, and they wish to save their souls, but they must also earn their living, and labor is now so organized that, without belonging to the organization, it is almost impossible to earn one's living."

This memorial was, of course, a confidential document. However, an enterprising correspondent for the *New York Herald* managed to get a shortened version, perhaps, as Archbishop Ireland said, "by bribing some secretary." The story appeared in the *Herald* and was picked up by the leading papers of America and Europe. Congratulatory cablegrams and newspaper comment, most of it favorable, poured in to the cardinal.

The Holy Office made a decision eighteen months later. The judgment read, *"Tolerari possunt"* — the Knights may be tolerated, under the condition that socialistic-sounding phrases be deleted from the constitution. Cardinal Gibbons wrote to Cardinal Simeoni, "I am very glad that the Holy Office has settled the affair with such an opinion, for it brings peace to souls, preserves the authority of Holy Church, and aids the salvation of many in the United States."

Four years later, in 1891, Pope Leo XIII published his encyclical *Rerum Novarum*, on the condition of the working class. It was the Church's first social encyclical. It gave the Church's authoritative ruling on the rights and duties of capital and labor. About the encyclical, the noted Cardinal Henry Edward Manning of England wrote to Gibbons, "We little thought when we were writing about the Knights in Rome a few years ago that every word would soon be published to the world by an emperor and a pope. Were we prophets?"

Cardinal Gibbons was justifiably proud of his work and accomplishments in connection with the Knights of Labor. Near the end of his life, he spoke of three of his experiences that were the most memorable. They were the Civil War, the Vatican Council, and the fight for the Knights of Labor. Historian Father John Tracy Ellis wrote, "Of all the many distinguished services which Cardinal Gibbons rendered to his Church and his country, the championship of the Knights of Labor won for him the most enduring fame and the most grateful remembrance."

———

Cardinal Gibbons was a friend of half a dozen United States presidents. In addition to Presidents Taft and Roosevelt, who, as we have seen, honored him at his anniversary as a priest and cardinal, he knew Grover Cleveland, Benjamin Harrison, William McKinley, and Woodrow Wilson.

Gibbons conferred with Cleveland over the Knights of Labor issue and joined with him in sending a copy of the United States

Constitution to Pope Leo XIII to honor him on his golden jubilee as a priest. Cleveland and his wife entertained Gibbons at a reception at the White House. The president attended the cornerstone-laying ceremony when Gibbons dedicated The Catholic University of America. Soon the friendship between the president and the cardinal came to the attention of the strongly anti-Catholic American Protective Association, or APA. It declared that when Cleveland became president he "had installed in the White House a wire to the cardinal's palace." Cleveland replied:

> I know Cardinal Gibbons and know him to be a good citizen and first-rate American, and that his kindness of heart and toleration are in striking contrast to the fierce intolerance and vicious malignity which disgrace some who claim to be Protestants.

It was true, as the APA implied in attacking Cleveland, that he and Gibbons were friendly. President Cleveland both entertained the cardinal and confided in him. Toward the end of his first term, while he was working on a message to Congress recommending a reduction in the tariff, Cleveland read the message to Gibbons and asked for his opinion. The cardinal paused reflectively for a moment and then praised the president for his frankness and statesmanship. "But I fear, Mr. President," he added, "that it will produce grave political complications." The prediction was accurate. At least partly as a result of the tariff message, Cleveland was defeated in the next election by Benjamin Harrison, who, in turn, was beaten by Cleveland four years later.

Gibbons was also on pleasant terms with Harrison, although not as close as with Cleveland. When the issue of Cahenslyism was dividing the Catholics in the country (Cahenslyism was a movement by German immigrants to set up their own German Catholic Church in America and is discussed in detail in the chapter about Archbishop Ireland), both President Harrison and Cardinal Gibbons happened to vacation at Cape May, New Jersey, at the same time. Meeting accidentally on the boardwalk, President Harrison invited the cardinal to his cottage where they discussed Cahensly-ism and the national agitation it was causing. Cardinal Gibbons had recently spoken on the subject in an attempt to defeat the movement among German nationals, and Harrison told him, "I had thought several times of writing to you and offering my congratulations on the remarks you made, but I refrained from doing so lest I should be interfering in Church matters." Gibbons relayed the president's feelings on this subject to Vatican officials, and this had a great deal to do with the final judgment on the matter.

President McKinley, like his predecessor Cleveland, had confidence in Gibbons' judgment. Following the Spanish-American War, which Gibbons had vainly tried to avert, McKinley found himself in a dilemma about the status of the Philippine Islands won from Spain. Should the United States retain the islands as its possession or grant them independence? McKinley summoned Gibbons to the White House and asked him, "Your Eminence, in your opinion, should the United States retain its hold over the Philippines?"

After considering the question, Gibbons felt that he had to be frank about his feelings. "Mr. President," he answered, "it would be a good thing for the Catholic Church, but, I fear, a bad one for the United States." He felt this way because he was convinced that the Church would prosper best under the American flag, but he thought that the United States should not become a colonial power with the difficulties and troubles this could bring.

After President McKinley was killed by an assassin's bullet, Theodore Roosevelt became president, and Gibbons formed a warm friendship with him also. Roosevelt and Gibbons — the ebullient Rough Rider and the small, mild prince of the Church — worked together over the settlement of the "Friars' Land" in the Philippines — four hundred thousand acres of rich farm land that had been acquired by four orders of Spanish monks resident there. Roosevelt felt such an admiration for the quiet and resourceful cardinal that he once enthusiastically exclaimed, "There is only one man in this country who has the nerve to get up and speak the truth. That man is Cardinal Gibbons."

The huge William Howard Taft, who towered over the cardinal, often sought Gibbons' help and enjoyed his company. Indeed, on President and Mrs. Taft's silver wedding anniversary, Gibbons was invited to dine with them as part of their family. It must have been difficult for Gibbons to vote in the election of 1912, when Taft and Roosevelt opposed Woodrow Wilson. Not even his good friend Archbishop Ireland could learn whether he voted for Taft or Roosevelt.

Although not on the same intimate terms with Wilson as with his five predecessors, Gibbons did call on the new president shortly after his first inauguration. Later, when the United States entered World War I, Gibbons followed up Wilson's war message by appealing to all citizens for "an absolute and unreserved obedience to his country's call." He then called a meeting of the archbishops of the country, who drafted a statement assuring the president of their unqualified support. On his birthday that year, Gibbons urged those entering the armed forces, "Be Americans always. Remember that you owe all to America and be prepared, if your country demands it, to give all in return."

When World War I was over, the cardinal was quick to urge support for Wilson's proposal for a League of Nations because it "will give us a reasonable guarantee against the horrors of war and a well-grounded assurance of peace, without impairing American sovereignty or surrendering any American right, and without involving us in entangling alliances."

To this endorsement, Wilson replied, "You have perceived, as is habitual with you, the really profound interests of humanity and of Christianity which are involved." When Wilson was preparing to go to Paris for the peace conference in 1918, Gibbons urged him to visit the pope while in Europe. Wilson did so — the first American president to officially visit a pope.

By the end of 1920, Cardinal Gibbons was beginning to feel that death was on the way. He was now 86 and had arteriosclerosis. On December 9, he celebrated his last Mass, and from then until he died, he spent most of his time in bed. His mind, however, remained alert, and it was reported that he asked one of his priests to read to him from the book *The Constitutional and Political History of the United States*, by Herman E. von Holst. On Washington's Birthday, February 22, 1921, he issued his final statement for the *Catholic Review* of Baltimore, and it was typical of the man that it should exult in the greatness of his beloved United States:

> As the years go by I am more than ever convinced that the Constitution of the United States is the greatest instrument of government that ever issued from the hand of man. That within the short space of one hundred years we have grown to be a great nation is due to the Constitution, the palladium of our liberties and the landmark in our march of progress.

Toward evening of the Wednesday of Holy Week, the cardinal awoke to find one of his priests with him. "My boy, I shall die tomorrow," he told him, and he asked to make his last confession. On Holy Thursday morning at 11:30, the cardinal died.

Tributes to the great cardinal poured in from all over the world. The pope, kings, statesmen and religious leaders all tried to express the loss they felt. Former President Taft, who was soon to become Chief Justice of the United States, said: "He did not belong to the Catholic Church alone, but he belonged to the country at large. He was Catholic not only in the religious sense but in the secular sense."

The New York Times, which did not always agree with him, editorialized, "He was one of the wisest men in the world."

Historian Theodore Maynard said of him, "He was the most influential and widely loved prelate that America has ever produced."

Archbishop John Ireland

Any immigrant who does not thank God that he is an American should in simple consistence take his foreign soul to foreign shores and crouch in misery and abjection beneath tyranny's scepter.

— *ARCHBISHOP JOHN IRELAND*

CHAPTER 5

Archbishop John Ireland

There have been many deeply patriotic American Catholic prelates, but the prize for the most outspoken in the history of the United States undoubtedly goes to Archbishop John Ireland of St. Paul, Minnesota. He was vigorously pro-American; he was proud of it, and he had not the slightest patience with anybody who was not. Fearless, powerful, oratorical, impetuous — he managed to get himself in trouble time and again with his fellow bishops or with Rome because of his outspoken manner. Sometimes he had to rely on his friend Cardinal James Gibbons to to get him out of trouble.

Toward the close of the nineteenth century, bishops in the United States were split neatly into two schools of thought on questions of nationalism and education. Liberals, or Americanizers, were progressive and in full sympathy with the American way, while the conservatives were more tradition-minded and wanted to follow the European pattern. Archbishop Ireland was leader of the liberals.

Much of the battle between these two sides was fought on nationalistic grounds — the Irish versus the Germans. Both groups had immigrated to the United States by the thousands in the 1880s, but the Germans weren't as quick to Americanize as the Irish were. They kept their own language and customs and gathered clannishly in large cities or in farming areas of the Midwest. This group resented the Irish "domination" of the Catholic Church in the United States, observing that there were twice as many Irish bishops as there were German bishops.

The Irish, on the other hand, were proud of the fact that they accepted the American way of life, spoke English, and mingled with other Americans. Church leaders like Cardinal Gibbons and Archbishop Ireland considered it important that Catholics become Americanized so the Church would not be considered a foreign institution. Archbishop Ireland felt strongly that the Germans should be compelled to speak English and abandon their national customs.

Archbishop Ireland first became involved in this controversy between the Germans and the Irish in 1886 when a priest by the name of Father P.M. Abbelen of Milwaukee, Wisconsin, presented a memorial to the Holy See asking that German parishes in the United States be altogether independent. For the sake of his argument he divided priests in the United States into German and Irish, and claimed that the Irish priests were considered the lawful pastors of all those born in America while German priests were regarded as merely necessary for the care of Catholics who spoke only the German language. "Are the Irish so much better than the Germans that they should have greater privileges?" he asked. The memorial requested the assignment of immigrants and their children to churches of their own language and an admonition to bishops and priests not to try to suppress foreign languages or customs.

This memorial was presented to the Holy See while Archbishop Ireland and Bishop John J. Keane were in Rome trying to lay the groundwork for the establishment of a Catholic university in the United States. Archbishop Ireland immediately presented a counter-memorial protesting against the insinuation that there was a conflict of races in America between the Germans and Irish. He said that there was no attempt to establish an Irish Church or Irish parishes, and if the Germans were permitted separate churches, other nationalities would request the same thing, leaving the Church in America without unity, life, or power.

Ireland's memorial recounted the many ways the Germans had been attempting to Germanize the Church and the ill effects that had come of these attempts: the tendency to regard the Church as an alien institution, the refusal of parents to send their children to

Catholic schools where only German was spoken, the alienation of Americans because they could not understand sermons in German, and the lack of hope for the conversion of American Protestants because of the language problem. Then the memorial stated that the Church "must be presented in a form attractive to Americans. The great objection which they have until now urged against her ... is that the Catholic Church is composed of foreigners, that it exists in America as an alien institution, and that it is, consequently, a menace to the existence of the Republic."

When the Vatican answered the memorials on April 5, 1888, it rejected the main points requested by Father Abbelen, declaring that the "Sacred Congregation of the Propaganda will never consider these petitions."

That, however, did not end the problem. The German resistance to Americanization soon took the name of Cahenslyism, named for Peter Paul Cahensly, a German merchant who was secretary general of the St. Raphael Society, a group that had been formed for the spiritual and material protection of German Catholic immigrants. Cahensly proposed a plan that would in essence establish a separate German Catholic Church in the United States, to be ruled by German-speaking bishops and priests. He presented his plan to Pope Leo XIII in April 1891 without first consulting the American hierarchy.

The outcry from Archbishop Ireland was thunderous. He lashed out at Cahensly's "impudence in undertaking under any pretext to meddle in the Catholic affairs in America." With his long white hair flowing over his powerful shoulders, his eyes flashing and his rock-like chin outthrust, the "consecrated blizzard from St. Paul" made it clear that "we are *American* bishops, and an effort is made to dethrone us and to foreignize our country in the name of religion."

Archbishop Ireland then went on the attack. He was determined to stir up public opinion against Cahenslyism. At the same time, he urged Cardinal Gibbons to use his influence to see to it that the Cahensly plan was rejected in Rome. Gibbons, however, following his usual policy of waiting for developments rather than jumping into a fight only half-prepared, waited until June to make his first statement on the subject. Then he pointed out that there were a vast number of churches in the United States established for Catholics of foreign birth and that he was therefore astonished that "a number of self-constituted critics and officious gentlemen in Europe" could complain that the Church was not taking proper care of the foreign population.

Soon after this speech, Cardinal Gibbons had occasion to discuss Cahenslyism with President Benjamin Harrison while the cardinal and the president were both vacationing at the same place. Learning that the president was concerned about the foreign influence of Cahenslyism, Gibbons relayed this information to the Vatican.

Finally, the Church authorities in Rome rejected the Cahensly plan. The papal secretary of state, Cardinal Rampolla, told Cardinal Gibbons that Pope Leo XIII "finds that plan neither opportune nor necessary."

The Germans, however, still were not ready to admit defeat. In September of 1892, a large convention of German Catholic societies met in Newark, New Jersey. They formally repudiated the attacks against Cahensly for "their evident absurdity and falseness, especially when they are hidden under the cover of patriotism and even devotion to the Holy See."

Americans were outraged. *The New York Times* editorialized, "We do not recall any other body of American residents, and presumably of American citizens, which has shown itself so completely out of touch with American institutions, not only because they are American, but because they are modern." The paper praised those churchmen "who were trying to persuade their countrymen of other beliefs that a devout Catholic may be as good a citizen as if he were not a Catholic. Among these are Cardinal Gibbons and Archbishop Ireland — yet these patriotic and devoted churchmen are the objects of a peculiar animosity on the part of the men at Newark."

Cahenslyism did eventually die out, and Germans became loyal American citizens who proved their devotion to the United States during World War I. For this, Catholic Americans should be eternally grateful to Archbishop Ireland. While most bishops felt as he did, he bore the brunt of the Cahensly controversy. It can be said that he, together with Cardinal Gibbons, saved the Church from embarrassment and suspicion in 1917, when the United States entered the war. About this fact *The New York Times* stated in 1917:

> The Cahensly movement was a direct outgrowth of pan-Germanism. Many who recall the struggle in the '80s and '90s do not hesitate to say that it was due to Gibbons and Ireland more than any others in the United States that the country went to war with so great a degree of solidarity against the government of one of the great peoples from which the American nation sprang.

In the summer of 1890, Archbishop Ireland addressed the National Education Association in St. Paul. In his speech, he eulogized "the free school of America." "Withered be the hand that is raised in sign of its destruction!" he shouted and expressed regret that Catholics had to have parochial schools because "the state school is nonreligious — ignores religion. And in loyalty to their principles, Catholics cannot and will not accept a common Christianity."

The Third Plenary Council six years earlier had declared that every pastor should erect a parochial school whenever possible to care for the religious education of the children. This, of course, meant then, as it does today, that Catholics would have to pay for their parochial schools while at the same time they were taxed for public schools they did not use.

Characteristically, Archbishop Ireland had a solution, and he put it into effect in two cities of his archdiocese, Faribault and Stillwater, Minnesota. Under his "Faribault Plan," the parochial schools were leased by the local school board between 9:00 and 3:45. Regular instruction was provided during those hours by nuns, who held state teacher licenses and whose salaries were paid as in any public school. Then, after 3:45, the nuns gave religious instruction to the pupils.

When Archbishop Ireland first proposed this arrangement, the effect was electrifying — even though the plan was not original with Ireland and was also in effect in Poughkeepsie, Boston, Cleveland, Hartford, and Savannah. Many Catholics were convinced that this "anti-Christ of the North" was out to destroy the parochial schools and turn them over to the "godless" public schools. As one writer said, it was not so much the proposal that his enemies found objectionable, "but it was the manner of the man — the proud, aggressive, fearless air with which he spoke. It was the firebrand hurling defiance even as he strove to do good that evoked an irate and immediate response."

Actually, a great deal of misunderstanding caused Archbishop Ireland's troubles, and they were magnified because at the time he was in his controversy over nationalism in the Church in the United States. The speech before the NEA was misunderstood because it was quoted out of context. He had indeed praised the public schools when he said: "Free schools! Blest indeed is the nation whose vales and hillsides they adorn, and blest the generations upon whose souls are poured their treasures." He had prefaced his remarks about the public schools by pointing out that the care of the child's mind is committed to the parents and by emphasizing the fact that tens of thousands of children would remain uninstructed if the task of their education rested solely on the parents. This was the reason he praised the free schools, because without them universal instruction would be impossible.

Archbishop Ireland also declared his belief in compulsory education, another part of the speech that was criticized because many thought that he was advocating compulsory education in state schools. He was not, however, as he made clear in his speech when he said that the parent "possesses the right to educate his child in the manner agreeable to himself, provided always that the education given in this manner suffices to fit the child for his ulterior duties to society."

Further, Archbishop Ireland's statement that "I repeat my regret that there is the necessity for its (the parochial school's) existence" was taken out of context, and he was accused of opposing parochial schools and reported to Rome. Actually, he meant that if the state schools were properly organized and if they granted to Catholic children all that was needed so far as the teaching of religion was concerned, there would be no need for parochial schools.

Those who criticized Archbishop Ireland ignored, or didn't take the trouble to find out, that two-thirds of the speech gave his reasons for dissatisfaction with public schools. He was dissatisfied, he said, because they made no provision for the teaching of religion. Lessons in religion at home or in Sunday school could not, he said, make up for this lack of religion, which could be taught more effectively in school. He said the religion the people learned at public school "was not the religion that built up our Christian civilization in the past ... It is not the religion that will guard the family and save society. It is manifest that dissatisfaction exists with the state school because of its exclusion of religion. This dissatisfaction, founded on conscience, will continue until the cause of it is removed."

It was no honor to America, he said, that ten million of its people were forced by law to pay taxes for the support of schools to which their conscience did not give approval; that they were, furthermore, compelled by their zeal for the religious instruction of their children to build schools of their own and to pay their own teachers. It was no honor to the American republic that she, more than any other nation, was eager to keep religion away from the schools. It was a terrible experiment upon which the nation had entered, he said, and "the very life of our civilization and of our country is at stake." At this point Archbishop Ireland proposed the Faribault Plan — also known as the Poughkeepsie Plan.

His speech should have been praised, but Archbishop Ireland's enemies in the Church were quick to grab at only the portions that praised the public schools, and a torrent of abuse fell on the archbishop. In the 1890s, it was the fashion among Catholic leaders to denounce public schools as "hotbeds of vice" and "sources of corruption." So, Archbishop Ireland was delated to Rome. His proposal was sent to the Vatican for critical examination together with "baskets of papers" attacking him for disobeying the rulings of the Third Plenary Council.

Cardinal Gibbons immediately came to his friend's defense. He wrote of Ireland:

> He is really a power and has more public influence than half a dozen of his neighbors. Such a man should not be under a cloud. There is no prelate in the United States who has done more to elevate and advance the Catholic religion. Protestants and Catholics alike almost idolize him. The circulation of even a rumor that his course is disapproved by the Holy See would do immense mischief to religion. The representations against him were doubtless made by parties who are narrow and do not understand the country in which they live.

The irrepressible John Ireland thanked Cardinal Gibbons for this defense, but also declared, "I rather enjoy the predicament into which I have got." Gibbons, however, who had such a completely different personality from Archbishop Ireland, did not share this enjoyment. He wrote a formal ten-page defense of the Minnesota archbishop to Pope Leo XIII.

Gibbons pointed out to the pope that it would always be necessary for some Catholic children to attend public schools but that these schools were not like those in other countries that did not teach religion because of opposition to religion. Instead, the American public schools didn't teach religion "in order not to offend the sentiments of the children who attend them and the parents who send them there. The care of providing the religious education of the children is left to the Church and to the Protestant sects."

The cardinal's defense emphasized that Archbishop Ireland was trying to end those divisions between Catholics and other Americans that had been caused by the false impression "that the Catholic Church is opposed in principle to the institutions of the country and that a sincere Catholic cannot be a loyal citizen of the United States." He continued:

> Catholics are not against state schools in principle; they recognize the great success of these schools; they desire neither their suppression nor diminution; what they ask is that the defects of the system be corrected, that religious teaching be given the place it is entitled to, in particular that Catholics be given the guarantee demanded by their conscience in the most important task of the education of their children.

Gibbons then invited Ireland to defend his plan before the annual meeting of the archbishops of the United States in St. Louis. As the cardinal later wrote: "After Ireland's explanation and his answers, not one of the archbishops offered a word of blame; many were explicit in approval."

Then, in January 1892, Ireland sailed for Rome to defend himself to the pope in person. After he submitted a long memorial in his defense, the pope took the matter out of the routine of the congregations and appointed a special commission of five cardinals to consider it. When this commission had reached its decision, the pope asked that the decision be brought to him at once. He interrupted his audiences, approved the decision, and expressed his joy that John Ireland had been vindicated. "*Tolerari potest*" (It may be tolerated), the decision read.

At once Ireland rejoiced: "The so-called Faribault Plan is now formally allowed in spite of Germans and Jesuits," while his enemies claimed victory in the dispute because the plan was only "tolerated," not "approved." But by this time the arrangements in Faribault and Stillwater had been canceled, primarily because of local opposition, both Catholic and Protestant.

During this controversy, many personal attacks were leveled at Archbishop Ireland, both in this country and in Rome. The attacks also brought forth tributes, the most notable of which appeared in the *Moniteur de Rome*. This article told of Ireland's efforts to extend the influence of the Church, to follow Catholic tradition in not allowing himself to be impeded by abandoned notions, to place religion above party politics, and to win souls to the Church. But the article was most notable because it was inspired by the pope himself, who had it written under his own eyes and, after revising it, sent it directly to the publication with instructions that it be printed *tel quel* (as is).

———

Despite how one might feel about Archbishop Ireland's impetuosity, which served to get him into trouble time and again during his life, it would be hard to find a man more devoted to American freedom. He was even brash enough to preach these ideas in Paris, France, where he urged the support of French Catholics to the Third Republic. He boasted of the American system of government as "the Church's happy self-government under a Constitution which makes Caesarism impossible."

Educated in France, John Ireland spoke French fluently (a talent envied by Cardinal Gibbons) and was "the pet of the French republicans." Gibbons complimented him on his talk: "It was a hazardous undertaking to fight for republicanism in a foreign tongue before an audience largely unfriendly."

Archbishop Ireland also participated in partisan politics, undoubtedly to a greater extent than any other American bishop in the history of the United States. He was an ardent Republican and didn't hesitate to attend Republican rallies. This was to precipitate one of the many crises in his life.

During the elections of 1894, Ireland appeared at Republican rallies in New York City. This "invasion" of the Archdiocese of New York was deeply resented by Archbishop Michael Corrigan and by

Bishop Bernard J. McQuaid of Rochester. The latter was so aroused that he denounced Archbishop Ireland from the pulpit of the Rochester cathedral while clad in his full episcopal robes and brandishing his crosier. During the sermon, Bishop McQuaid announced that in order to keep the holy office of bishop free from entanglements with any political party, he himself had refrained from voting for the past twenty-seven years.

There was no way a man like Archbishop Ireland could keep from responding to that attack. He didn't reply at once, however, but waited a few months until he delivered an address on "American Citizenship" in Chicago. "Any American who refuses to vote deserves disfranchisement or exile!" he roared, and later wrote gleefully to Cardinal Gibbons, "People were wicked enough to see in these words an allusion to His Lordship of Rochester."

Cardinal Gibbons, who considered voting a civic duty but who never revealed his choice of party or candidate, in the meantime had notified the papal secretary of state of the "disgraceful" attack of Bishop McQuaid on his brother bishop. Bishop McQuaid was rebuked for "this deplorable incident."

———•———

Bishop Ireland first gained national attention as a vigorous patriot at the Third Council of Baltimore, which opened on November 10, 1884. He already had a reputation as a powerful orator and was, therefore, invited to give an address. He selected as his topic "The Catholic Church and Civil Society." He recognized the fact that the eyes of the country were focused on what was happening in Baltimore, so he felt that they wanted to hear a statement about the attitude of the Church toward the form of government found in the United States. He said:

> There is no conflict between the Catholic Church and America. I could not utter one syllable that would belie, however remotely, either the Church or the Republic, and when

I assert, as I now solemnly do, that the principles of the Church are in thorough harmony with the interests of the Republic, I know in the depths of my soul that I speak the truth.

He preached on the doctrines of the Church as they related to civil authority and showed how the Church, throughout its history, had fought for liberty — liberty for herself, personal liberty against slavery, and civil liberty against encroachments of sovereigns. Then he concluded with these inspiring words:

Republic of America, receive from me the tribute of my love and of my loyalty. With my whole soul I do thee homage. I pray from my heart that thy glory be never dimmed. *Esto perpetua* (Let it be perpetual). Thou bearest in thy hands the hope of the human race; thy mission from God is to show to nations that men are capable of highest civil and political liberty. Be thou ever free and prosperous. Through thee may liberty triumph over the earth from the rising to the setting sun. *Esto perpetua*. Believe me, no hearts love thee more ardently than Catholic hearts, no tongues speak more honestly thy praises than Catholic tongues, and no hand will be lifted up stronger and more willing to defend, in war and in peace, thy laws and thy institutions than Catholic hands. *Esto perpetua*.

Archbishop Ireland was extremely proud of his American citizenship. He considered the United States a providential nation whose mission it is to prepare the world for human liberty. Hence, he believed that American liberty must be preserved as the one thing on earth most sacred, for "when it is quenched, there is no other ray of light toward which common man may turn his face." Time and again he professed his love for God and country:

When the question is asked, "Do you put Church before country or country before Church?" I say that one is not to be put before the other. They are in different spheres altogether, and so far as principle goes, the Church tells me that service to the state and country is a solemn, sacred, religious duty. I do not think that anyone is fit to enter the kingdom of heaven who is not capable of taking care of, so far as the opportunity affords, this magnificent kingdom given us here, the republic of America.

At Archbishop John Hennessy's jubilee in Dubuque, Iowa, on October 18, 1891, responding to the toast "Church and country," he said, "Church and country; soul and body; the one is necessary to the other, and there is no distinction between the love we owe to the one and that which the other demands."

The archbishop spoke so many times on the subject of American liberty that it is impossible to do him justice in this chapter alone. His discourses before the New York Commandery of the Legion on April 4, 1894; his address on American citizenship before the Union League of Chicago on Washington's Birthday, 1895; his address on the American republic before the Marquette Club of Chicago on October 7, 1899, in the presence of President McKinley; his address on Abraham Lincoln before the Lincoln Club of Chicago, February 12, 1903; speeches delivered in Sioux City, Omaha, Boston, St. Louis, and other cities — all of these throbbed with the purest patriotism. No wonder that when a visiting minister at a certain church in St. Paul preached on the Catholic Church as the enemy of America, he was reminded that "the biggest Republican" in America was Archbishop John Ireland.

————

Archbishop Ireland didn't just talk about patriotism. He had proven himself on the battleground when he served as a chaplain during the Civil War — the chaplain of the first regiment in the United States to respond to President Lincoln's call for the defense of the Union.

John Ireland was born in Burnchurch, Kilkenny, Ireland, on September 11, 1838, to Richard and Judith Naughton Ireland. The family moved to America in 1849, lived in Boston and Chicago, then settled in St. Paul, Minnesota, in 1853. Bishop Joseph Cretin, the first bishop of St. Paul, sent him to France to study for the priesthood at Meximieux and at the Marist Seminary; he was ordained by Bishop Thomas Grace on December 21, 1861.

In March 1862, the new Father Ireland, who had volunteered for the army, received his commission as a chaplain. The regiment was sent to the South to fight under General Rosecrans. It distinguished itself in the Battle of Corinth by saving the day for the North. A picture of that battle is today in the Minnesota state capitol. The picture gives Father Ireland a place of honor because, during the battle, when ammunition was beginning to run low, the priest had hurried down the line, heedless of the bullets flying around him, and had carried a supply of ammunition to the men, crying, "Here are your cartridges, boys, don't spare them!"

According to others in the regiment, Ireland soon became one of the most popular officers in the regiment, for he endured all the hardships of the men and kept their spirits up with a ready smile and words of encouragement. He was a good chess player, too, and carried a little chess set with him so he could divert the attention of at least one man during a game of chess.

The *Herald* of Utica, New York, quoted the reminiscence of a veteran who had been wounded at the battle of Corinth. As he lay on the battlefield, a man came to him, knelt beside him, made him drink from his flask, and dressed his wounds. When he asked the name of the benefactor who saved his life, he learned that it was John Ireland. This was no isolated incident. Major I. R. Holcomb described similar incidents in an article for the *St. Paul Pioneer Press*.

After the war, Father Ireland joined the Grand Army of the Republic and it was said that during G.A.R. reunions no name was more warmly cheered than that of the Minnesota chaplain. He was elected chaplain-in-chief of the G.A.R. in 1906. He was also elected an honorary member of the Veteran Corps of the Sixty-Ninth Regiment (the Fighting Sixty-Ninth). He was never happier than when greeting old soldiers, and he took special pride in his companionship with those who, like himself, wore the Medal of Honor.

Ireland was unable to finish the war as a chaplain. His health broke and he was forced to return to St. Paul. He assumed duties as assistant to the pastor of the cathedral and then became rector of the cathedral on July 28, 1867. During the time he was at the cathedral he was a vigorous shepherd of souls and took special interest in temperance work. He founded the Total Abstinence Society in 1869, the beginning of a nationwide movement against intemperance.

Father Ireland represented his bishop at the First Vatican Council. There he met a young bishop from North Carolina, Bishop James Gibbons, and a friendship developed that was to last the rest of his life. In 1875, Ireland was named coadjutor bishop of St. Paul. He succeeded Bishop Grace, who had ordained him, when Bishop Grace resigned in 1884. In 1888, when his see became an archdiocese, he became its first archbishop.

———•———

One of the projects closest to Archbishop Ireland's heart was the movement to colonize Minnesota. It has been said that among all the enterprises of the archbishop, "There was none that so cruelly taxed his energies as did the colonization movement — none that caused him so much anxiety of soul."

Behind this movement were two motives: to afford relief to the unemployed thousands in the large eastern cities, and to offer a home to European immigrants who were fleeing from famine and oppression — particularly from Ireland. In 1850, the United States census showed nine hundred sixty-one thousand Irish-born people in the population of the country, forty-four percent of the foreign-born population of the entire nation. During the next ten years, another million people fled from Ireland.

Most of the immigrants settled in the cities on the eastern seaboard and tried to find work among the unskilled labor. Living conditions were deplorable and the mortality rate so high that during the great famine it was said that two-thirds of the Irish died three years after reaching this country. The mortality rate explains why the first charitable institutions erected in dioceses in those days were always orphanages.

Bishop Ireland's solution to this problem was to bring the Irish immigrants to the western states where they could start farms. He felt that if the suffering poor in the large cities could be brought to the almost limitless land in the West, the labor question could be largely solved. So, in 1864, the Minnesota Irish Emigration Society was launched in St. Paul with then-Father Ireland as its president. In 1876, Bishop Ireland founded the Catholic Colonization Bureau of Minnesota, and the next year he founded the Catholic Colonization Land Stock Company.

By September of 1877, the bishop was able to report that eight hundred entries had been made on one hundred seventeen thousand acres of government land available for settlement under preemption and homestead acts and about sixty thousand acres of land procured from railroads had been occupied. This was only a start. From then on, the archbishop was responsible for establishing many communities of immigrants on rich, free lands or cheap railroad lands on long terms. These immigrants would be brought to Minnesota and provided with supplies until they were able to raise a crop.

Although this operation was of extreme importance to John Ireland and the Church in Minnesota, its details are not in the scope of this book. Suffice it to say that Archbishop Ireland was mainly responsible for establishing thriving villages and happy homes over hundreds of thousands of acres on the prairies of Minnesota.

—·—

Archbishop Ireland was a fighter. When he believed in something he would fight for it all the way. His letters were filled with fighting words or metaphors using military terms. This was especially true during the "Americanism" controversy that is discussed in the chapter about Father Isaac Hecker. Unable to be present at a meeting of the United States archbishops because of other engagements, Ireland wrote that he regretted that he was not there "as I am anxious to break a lance against all comers in defense of Heckerism."

In the same letter (which was sent to Paulist Father Walter Elliott), Ireland admitted, "I like to fight and conquer with few allies. You owe nothing, or but little, when the victory is won." He said that he had received a letter from Cardinal Rampolla, "written on the field itself — the Vatican," thus likening the Vatican to a battlefield during the "war" over Americanism.

This willingness of Ireland to jump into battle to defend himself, or the things in which he believed, could be considered either a virtue or a vice. Certainly it showed that he had the courage of his convictions and would stand up for them no matter what the odds, but his impetuosity also got him into trouble.

There was a tremendous difference between the characters and personalities of Archbishop Ireland and Cardinal Gibbons in this respect. Gibbons' philosophy was to do nothing unless absolutely necessary. He undoubtedly was much more prudent than Ireland, but he could also be accused of vacillation at times. However, as we have seen, when Gibbons considered it necessary to speak and give his opinion, he did so with complete fearlessness.

The differences between Ireland and Gibbons were described this way by Ireland's biographer James H. Moynihan:

> Gibbons was an admirable foil for Ireland, tempering his enthusiasms with his natural conservatism, his daring with his prudence ... If at times Ireland's impetuosity and his readiness to engage in battle must have disturbed the cardinal's equanimity, the latter saw that behind it all was a passion for God and country, as well as an honesty and a sincerity of soul.

Archbishop Ireland sometimes became impatient with Cardinal Gibbons, often complaining in his correspondence with others, such as Bishop John J. Keane and Msgr. Denis O'Connell, that the cardinal waited too long to act. This was particularly so in the fight over Cahenslyism, when Ireland was doing all he could to bring a condemnation of Cahensly while Gibbons preferred to wait to see what action Rome would take. To Ireland's continued urgings for action, Gibbons pointed out that the displeasure of President Harrison and Harrison's words of rebuke to German nationalism would have more weight in Rome "than the combined protests of the hierarchy."

Archbishop Ireland and Cardinal Gibbons have both been compared to politicians and statesmen. Gibbons' biographers, John and Arline Boucher, said of Gibbons, "In place of the politician's impatience for results, he showed the statesman's ability to wait," implying that Ireland was more the politician. When Gibbons did decide the time was right to speak, however, his words were listened to.

Another trait that made Ireland different from Gibbons was Ireland's love of a fight. Once a fight was started, Ireland liked to finish it, and this was true in the battle over German nationalism in the American Church, the controversy over education, and the fight about Americanism. In the case of the latter, Ireland tried to keep the issue alive by proposing at the annual meeting of the archbishops that every bishop in the country should be asked if he knew of the existence of this heresy and, if so, where it existed and who taught it. The vote on the proposal was a tie, which Cardinal Gibbons broke by voting against it. Gibbons wanted to bring this matter to a close, while Ireland wanted to win the fight. He wrote disgustedly to Msgr. O'Connell, "Baltimore cried 'Peace, peace, death even for the sake of peace,' and nothing was effected."

But the friendship between the archbishop and the cardinal grew ever stronger through the years. Ireland often thanked Gibbons for his support in his battles and for shielding him. He spoke at Gibbons' jubilee in 1893 and at the beginning of each year exchanged warm greetings with him.

Gibbons, for his part, also spoke glowingly about Archbishop Ireland. A few weeks after Archbishop Ireland's death, Cardinal Gibbons praised him as "the sturdy patriot who endeared himself to the American people without distinction of race or religion, the man who had contributed perhaps more than any other to demonstrate the harmony that exists between the constitution of the Church and the Constitution of the United States."

———•———

Archbishop Ireland served both his Church and his country in official capacities. It has been mentioned that he was brash enough to speak in Paris, France, about republicanism as it existed in the United States. That speech did not come about by accident.

After Ireland had fought and won the school controversy in Rome, Pope Leo XIII commissioned him to go to Paris to try to restore order in the Church there. The Catholics of France viewed the Third Republic as the enemy of Catholicism because of many measures that had been directed against the Church. The pope was doing all he could to rally the French Catholics to the Republic. He had sent a letter to the French people in February of 1892 urging them to accept the Republic and to unite for the protection of religion, but this effort seemed to have failed, even arousing resentment among old influential families.

Therefore Pope Leo asked Archbishop Ireland to see what he could do. Ireland arrived in Paris in June and arranged to speak on "Conditions in America" on June 18. He painted a glowing picture of life in the United States. He described American democracy as a form of government in keeping with the fundamental principles of Christianity and said that the Church was "a free Church in a free State" and told his listeners that the Republic granted complete liberty to the Church. He then suggested that France could achieve the same through the Third Republic: "Just now the Church is resolved to make trial in France of the Republic, and I, as a citizen of a republic, say to the Church: 'In this experiment thou shalt succeed.'"

The address was widely quoted in the French press, and Archbishop Ireland soon became a controversial personality in Paris. He was encouraged to make other speeches, and he did. He urged Catholic priests to get out and mingle with the people, something that was unheard of in France. He also told them that they should be in the forefront of the fight for improved working conditions:

> Go into the factories. See the awful conditions that are so often found there. See these men packed together in an atmosphere in which even an angel could not live. See their children, their young daughters, their wives, broken in health before their time by deplorable hygiene and overwork. Say, "In the name of Christ, in the name of humanity, this must be changed." Be the first apostles of social justice and the upholders of distributive justice.

Paper after paper reproduced his addresses. They also described his appearance, his habits, and his democratic ways. *Le Petit Journal*, for example, gave this portrait:

> Tall, well-built, his face a mixture of energy and sweetness, frank and refined, his look clear and penetrating, his voice warm, sonorous as brass, his speech fluent, at times familiar, at times lofty. Simply dressed, he wears no pectoral cross or evidence of his dignity, not even a watch chain. His old-fashioned trousers and large hobnailed shoes reveal a gentleman who does not frequent the best New York clothiers.

While in Paris, Ireland visited the Chamber of Deputies and made the acquaintance of many of its members. He also was received by President Carnot and members of his cabinet. He made such an impression that he received a letter from Cardinal Rampolla stating, "The Holy Father has been pleased with the regard shown you."

As Pope Leo XIII chose John Ireland to represent the Church, so President McKinley chose him to represent the United States. The archbishop was chosen in 1900 to deliver the address on the occasion of the presentation to France, by the youth of America, a statue of General Lafayette. McKinley told Ireland that he was chosen because "no more eminent representative of American eloquence and patriotism could have been chosen, and none could better give appropriate expression to the sentiments of gratitude and affection that bind our people to France."

The ceremony was one of unusual splendor. Present were the ambassador of the United States; the president of the Republic of France, M. Loubet; members of the French cabinet; the papal nuncio; and many other officials. John Phillip Sousa's band played the American and French national anthems. Then the archbishop spoke, extolling the relationship of America and France, thanking France for coming to the aid of the young nation at the time of the Revolutionary War and proclaiming Lafayette as the exemplar of true liberty.

Archbishop Ireland also represented the United States in 1909 at the festival of the centenary of Lafayette in Paris. The French people held the archbishop in high esteem. Among other honors, he was decorated as a commander of the Legion of Honor by the French ambassador to the United States at a ceremony in Paris.

———

On March 27, 1898, the pope asked Archbishop Ireland to see what he could do to prevent the Spanish-American War. He made the request through Archbishop John Keane, the first rector of The Catholic University of America, a close personal friend of Ireland who happened to be in Rome at the time. Keane cabled Ireland urging him to leave for Washington to see the president, informing him that the pope was using his influence with Spain, but could do nothing until he had heard from Archbishop Ireland.

When Archbishop Ireland received the cable, it was somewhat late to intervene, but he did what he could. He arranged to meet with President McKinley on April 1. Meanwhile, on March 29, McKinley proposed to Spain an armistice lasting until October 1 with negotiations to be held until then to preserve peace. On March 31, the Spanish government rejected this proposal and the president announced he would lay the matter before Congress on April 6.

The Spanish-American War was caused by the revolution in Cuba that began in 1895. The Spanish governor put down the revolution and herded the rebels into concentration camps. The American sympathies were with the rebels because Americans remembered their own struggle for independence. Besides, the spirit of nationalism was rampant, and men of great prominence — Theodore Roosevelt, Henry Cabot Lodge, Secretary John Hay, and Whitelaw Reid — were ardent advocates of war in order for the United States to take its place among the great powers of the world.

The desire for war was extremely strong among many elements in the United States at that time, especially after the battleship Maine was destroyed on February 15, 1898, with the loss of two hundred fifty-eight men. However, Ireland was able to report, after the April 1 meeting, that McKinley was ardently desirous of peace. On April 2, Ireland cabled Rome that he had met with the leaders in the Senate, that the war party in Congress was very strong and threatened to act against the will of the president.

On April 3, Archbishop Ireland met with the Spanish minister, Señor Polo, together with Senator Stephen B. Elkins. The two Americans impressed upon the Spanish minister that war was inevitable unless Spain asked for an armistice such as that proposed by President McKinley. After much discussion, the minister agreed to ask his government to propose a six-month armistice, and Archbishop Ireland cabled the pope to urge the Spanish government to take immediate action to request the armistice.

From this time until the declaration of war, the archbishop was in daily contact with Cardinal Rampolla urging again and again that he get from Spain a clear, definite proposal of armistice. Archbishop Ireland also met with representatives of France, Spain, Belgium, Austria, and Russia and received assurances of cooperation and promises of mediation. However, due to American belligerence as well as Spanish pride, such a request for armistice did not arrive until April 10.

With negotiations going on, McKinley, still hoping for peace, delayed sending his message to the Senate on April 6 in order to give

Spain time to act. However, on April 13, the Foreign Affairs Committee of the House of Representatives adopted a resolution calling on President McKinley to establish in Cuba an independent government and to use the army and navy for that purpose. McKinley still did not want war, but the pressures became too great. Newspapers yelped for war, and the demands of Congress became more and more insistent. Because of the determination of so many in Congress, war was declared.

Ireland naturally regretted his failure to prevent the war. However, historians have acknowledged that this failure was primarily due to his lack of time. Had he been called in to undertake the negotiations two months earlier, he could have been successful. He had been successful in delaying the president's message for four days in hope that the armistice might come. Senator C.K. Davis, who praised Ireland's "most arduous and incessant" labors for peace, wrote that, "If the armistice had been tendered one week earlier than it was, I think there would have been a settlement of all our questions with Spain without war." Once war was declared, Ireland supported his country, saying: "Now I am for war — for the Stars and Stripes. I am all right as an American."

It took considerable courage on John Ireland's part to enter these negotiations, for at the time he first went to Washington the cries for war were extremely insistent throughout the country. He was risking his reputation as an American patriot to try to avert war. He admitted that he was afraid that he would harm himself by going to Washington and that he did so only because of the repeated telegrams from Archbishop Keane. He knew that "I was risking my reputation as an American," but he was glad, too, to obtain a reputation for working for peace, even though unsuccessfully.

———•———

After the United States' victory over Spain, the Philippine Islands, won from Spain, caused numerous problems. Particularly troublesome were the Spanish friars and the land they owned. The United

States appointed two commissions to study the problem, one under William Howard Taft and the other under Dr. Jacob Gould Schurman of Cornell. These commissions concluded that, since under the Spanish rule these friars were practically the executive officers of the government, they were all that the Filipinos detested politically, so Filipino priests should replace them.

Taft's report stated that "the Augustinians, the Recollects, and the Dominicans owned four hundred thousand acres of land" which the Filipinos wanted for the Filipino Republic. Taft's report also pointed out that "so great was the political enmity, hostility, towards the friars, who opposed the revolution of 1896, that forty of them were slain and four hundred put under arrest."

To settle the problems of the Philippines and the Church, the pope wanted the United States to appoint a commission that would deal directly with the Vatican. Such an idea, however, seemed so at variance with American traditions that it was feared it would arouse bigotry in this country. Protestant religions would be up in arms against this recognition of the Vatican by the U.S. government.

Once more Pope Leo XIII called on Archbishop Ireland because of the friendly relations he had with both President McKinley and President Theodore Roosevelt. Archbishop Ireland was asked to negotiate the matter and for the next several years this mission occupied a great deal of his attention. Both the Vatican and the United States government relied heavily on his cooperation and counsel in all matters pertaining to the Philippines.

Archbishop Ireland was approached first in May of 1901 by Cardinal Rampolla, who wrote that he "must have direct relations with someone who would be in a position to let me know the wishes and the intentions of the American government." He acknowledged that the opposition to the establishment of diplomatic relations was formidable, so all he could hope for was for the president to give someone the mission of going to Rome to negotiate the Philippines affair. He told the archbishop that this was the mind of the pope and that

Ireland's "former accomplishments" led the cardinal to believe that the archbishop could best carry out the pope's wishes.

Archbishop Ireland first wrote to Taft telling him that the Vatican was ready to settle the matter of the friars' property. Taft replied that he approved of the idea of sending a commission to Rome. Ireland also kept in touch with President Roosevelt and impressed upon him the fact that the dispatching of the commission would be well-received on both sides of the ocean. The commission, headed by Taft, was appointed and went to Rome for negotiations in May of 1902.

Agreements were reached, but agreements that brought considerable criticism from certain portions of the Catholic Church in this country. This criticism came mainly because the United States government insisted on separation of Church and State in the Philippines, a condition that had not prevailed when the islands were under Spain. Ireland defended the government's position. He told of his audience with the pope, who expressed himself as well-pleased with the relation of the government to the Church in the islands. He said that the direction of Catholic affairs is the business of the pope and not irresponsible Church societies or newspaper editors.

Throughout the years of negotiations over the Philippines, Archbishop Ireland was in constant contact with everyone of importance in Washington and in the islands. He managed to maintain cordial relations with President Roosevelt and his administration and the hierarchy in the Philippines. Although he received considerable criticism from some who felt he was not vigorous enough in defending the friars, Ireland understood that the friars were unpopular in the Philippines, and Church authorities in Rome agreed with him that the best possible solutions to the problems were achieved.

———·———

John Ireland occupied a unique place in American affairs. There have been many exceptionally patriotic prelates in the history of the United States, but none took such an active part in public affairs as

Ireland. Able to wield immense influence, he was considered, in the words of Justice Pierce Butler, "a giant on the side of right in every crisis, in peace and war." President Theodore Roosevelt said, "Every true American should be glad that there lives in the United States so stout a champion of Americanism as Archbishop Ireland — the only bishop, by the way, in existence who is entitled to wear that badge of nobility, the button of the Loyal Legion."

During his years as a bishop, Ireland was friendly with all the presidents except Woodrow Wilson. He campaigned for McKinley in 1896 and 1900, and this president, in turn, appointed him to make the address at the presentation of the statue of Lafayette in 1900. McKinley also spoke warmly of Ireland, saying, "If we had more Irelands, we would have less sectarian rancor, and the Republic and the Catholic Church would alike be the gainers."

Archbishop Ireland's relations with Roosevelt and Taft were especially warm, particularly with Roosevelt, who once in Carnegie Hall called Ireland one of his most valued friends. Roosevelt claimed that he counted the opportunity of becoming friends with Ireland as one of the greatest benefits he had derived from being in Washington, that there was not a man in the country who deserved better of the nation or rendered better service to the people.

There is evidence that Roosevelt recognized a similarity between Ireland and himself. Writing to Ireland in September of 1898, Roosevelt said that he was tempted to begin the letter, "My dear comrade," for, "You are so true a comrade, so true a democrat, in the proper sense of the word, that I feel a right of comradeship with you, both as soldier and citizen." It is possible to find much similarity between the archbishop and the president; they had both distinguished themselves on the battlefield during war, were somewhat impetuous, loved a good fight, and were enemies of intemperance.

Archbishop Ireland was a frequent and welcome visitor at the White House during Roosevelt's tenure as president, and the archbishop's correspondence shows that his advice was frequently asked and acted upon. In the correspondence, too, are letters from Roosevelt thanking Ireland for "all you have done not merely for this administration, but for the American republic during the past few years." Roosevelt wrote that he wished he had five minutes to himself so that he could pay his respects to one "whom I am proud to hail as one of the greatest exemplars of American citizenship."

Archbishop Ireland's relations with Taft first began during the negotiations over the Philippines and developed into a fine understanding. After he was elected president, Taft wrote to Ireland thanking him for all that he had done during the campaign and expressed his satisfaction that many Catholics, normally Democrats, had voted for him. He assured Ireland that no one would receive a more cordial welcome in the White House than he would.

He was not, however, on friendly terms with President Wilson, who was noted for his unfriendliness toward the Catholic Church. The one time Archbishop Ireland went to the White House to pay his respects to Wilson, he was received with chilling courtesy, and the only letter he received from Wilson, of five lines, was also lacking in warmth. Of course, Ireland was a noted Republican while Wilson was a Democrat, which probably was much of the reason.

———•———

Archbishop Ireland died at the age of eighty, a little before 4:00 a.m. on September 25, 1918. The day of his funeral, the flag on City Hall in St. Paul flew at half-staff, and the flag on the state capitol was lowered in respect. The funeral procession was one of the largest ever witnessed in the United States, showing the respect and admiration in which his fellow citizens held Archbishop John Ireland.

Father Isaac Hecker

The republic of the United States, in affirming man's natural rights, started in the eighteenth century with its face to Catholicity and is in the ascending way of life to God.

— *FATHER ISAAC HECKER*

CHAPTER 6

Father Isaac Hecker

In 1897, Father Isaac Thomas Hecker had already been dead for nine years. Yet, indirectly, he was to be responsible for a heresy that went under the name of "Americanism" — a heresy that had to be condemned by the pope.

Please note in the above statement, however, that Hecker was *indirectly* responsible for this heresy. It is not accurate, and not at all fair, to place the blame for this heresy on the founder of the Paulist Fathers. It would be better to say that a *translation of a biography of Father Hecker* was responsible. In addition, the heresy of Americanism was really a "phantom heresy, which existed everywhere, anywhere, nowhere."

It was noted in the chapter about Archbishop Ireland that Pope Leo XIII had sent him to France to preach his progressive ideas and to try to encourage Catholics to support the Third Republic. Although Ireland spoke in 1892, by 1897 it was doubtful that these progressive ideas had made much progress in France.

Then Abbe Felix Klein, a professor at the Catholic Institute of France who greatly admired Father Hecker and the liberal American bishops, translated into French the book *The Life of Father Isaac Thomas Hecker*, which had been written in 1891 by Paulist Father Walter Elliott, with an introduction by Archbishop Ireland. Hecker praised the compatibility of American political institutions with the Catholic Church, and the French translation of the book was soon eagerly grabbed up by the French republicans to be used as a charter for their whole new approach to Church affairs under the Third Republic.

With the translation, Klein wrote a glowing, if somewhat inaccurate, preface to the book. He compared Hecker to Benjamin Franklin and Abraham Lincoln as self-made men, and compared him to St. Augustine in his travels toward Catholicism. He praised him as the ideal type of modern priest who could overcome Protestantism with new methods.

The French royalists immediately condemned the book as preaching heresy. They said that Hecker's method of winning converts was to water down doctrine to such an extent that Hecker was really a Protestant. Thus, a priest "who had lived in comparative obscurity in the United States" became the center of a religious battle in Europe nine years after his death.

Suddenly American bishops learned that French clergymen were condemning something called Americanism. They were dumbfounded. To them Americanism meant nothing more than love of country, and they couldn't imagine what the fuss was all about in France.

Msgr. Denis O'Connell, one of Cardinal Gibbons' closest confidants, was invited to speak on Americanism at the Fourth International Catholic Scientific Congress in Fribourg, Switzerland. In his talk, he carefully distinguished between the political meaning of the term and its meaning in the religious sense. He said that "political Americanism" was based chiefly on the Declaration of Independence and the Constitution, and he showed that the ideas in these documents were in agreement with the principles of the Catholic Faith because they recognize the dignity of man and the equality of persons. Explaining "ecclesiastical Americanism," O'Connell said that it was a practical solution to the relation between Church and State in the United States. In the United States, he said, the Church was allowed full freedom, which it would not have if there were an established Church.

O'Connell said that Hecker accepted both Americanisms — the political because he thought it was as good if not better than any other existing system, and the ecclesiastical because he could find nothing that served the Church better in America.

Then, in 1898, a new book was printed in France called *Is Father Hecker a Saint?* With its satirical title, it was an attack on Hecker by Abbe Charles Maignen — a malicious jumble of accusations and distortions. Since it had the imprimatur of Father Albert Lepidi, O.P., the master of the Sacred Palace in the Vatican (although Cardinal Richard of Paris had refused an imprimatur), it gave the impression that it had the approval of Rome.

This was too much for Cardinal Gibbons, as patient a man as he was. He wrote a strong letter to the Holy See protesting "this incriminating tendency," "perverse insinuations," and "revolting calumnies." The cardinal declared:

> I could hardly believe my eyes to read such atrocities. What do they mean when they talk about Americanism in relation to this episcopate and this clergy? Of course we love our country and are devoted to it; we like its institutions because they allow us our whole liberty for goodness and allow us to spread more and more the action of religion and the influence of the Church. If that were what they call Americanism, wherein is the harm?
>
> But no, they are using the word like a scarecrow; they want to suggest a perverse tendency of a doctrine not only suspicious, but clearly erroneous and even heretical. Well, I can guarantee that all this is false, unfair, slanderous. I have no hesitation in affirming that you have not in the whole world an episcopate, a clergy, and believers more fundamentally Catholic, firmer in their faith, and more devoted to the Holy See.

Archbishop Ireland, as can be imagined, had been in the thick of this fight from the beginning, since he had written the introduction to the English version of *The Life of Father Hecker*. Ireland had spoken in France in support of the Third Republic, so the French royalists were quick to involve him. Abbe Maignen, whose book *Is Father Hecker a Saint?* gave fullest impetus to the controversy, claimed that Ireland's visit to France "greatly contributed to spread and accelerate the movement." He claimed that Ireland was the future head of the schismatical American Church and that "the Ireland party is full of doctrinal audacity; it allies itself shamelessly with the Protestants against Catholics, and it has the support of the American government."

Ireland fought back with a nine-page letter to the cardinal secretary of state at the Vatican protesting the "calumnies, palpable exaggerations" in Maignen's book. He said that the book could do great harm in America because it criticized what the author called Americanism and, "For the American people the word Americanism is sacred, a symbol of everything they hold dear, their civil and political institutions."

He alluded to the fact that he himself had been accused of being "on the point of starting a schism" and emphasized that he and all other American bishops "have only one system — that of the Holy See; have only one kind of ideas — that of the Holy See. They (the bishops) obey the least word that comes from Rome. In what instance have we not followed the wish of the pope?"

By this time the issue was being debated throughout Europe, and newspapers were proclaiming: "Americanism condemned? Paulists are anathema! Gibbons, Keane, and Ireland under papal censure!" Yet the average American didn't even realize this conflict existed because the issue was hardly discussed in the American press.

Finally, Archbishop Ireland decided to go to Rome to defend himself and the Church in America. However, he arrived in Rome too late, because five days before his arrival Pope Leo XIII felt compelled to act. On January 22, 1899, he signed an encyclical addressed to "Our Beloved Son, James Cardinal Gibbons." This encyclical, *Testem Benevolentiae* ("Proof of Our Love"), condemned tendencies "which some comprise under the name of Americanism."

The pope's encyclical specifically mentioned some teachings found in the French edition of *The Life of Father Hecker*, such as overreliance on the Holy Ghost's individual guidance, the stressing of "natural" over "supernatural" virtues, the distinction between "active and passive" virtues, and the use of "new" methods of winning converts. But he also was careful to proclaim that he was not condemning the American spirit and that Americanism was not necessarily a doctrine accepted by Americans, but that he retained the name because it was so used in Europe.

Cardinal Gibbons was now obliged to formally reply to the letter. In doing so, he thanked Pope Leo for "having cast light on all these questions" and then continued:

> This doctrine, which I deliberately call extravagant and absurd, this Americanism, as it has been called, has nothing in common with the views, aspirations, doctrine, and conduct of Americans. I do not think that there can be found in the entire country a bishop, a priest, or even a layman with a knowledge of his religion who has ever uttered such enormities. No, this is not — it never has been and never will be — our Americanism. I am deeply grateful to Your Holiness for having yourself made this distinction in your Apostolic Letter.

Through private sources, Cardinal Gibbons learned that, although the encyclical was addressed to America, it was actually aimed at France, where, because of the encyclical, French Americanism had faded almost overnight.

Archbishop Ireland also answered the pope's letter. He said:

> Today the light has been shed abroad and misunderstandings cease. Now we can scotch the error which some have wished to cloak under the name of Americanism, and we can define the truth which alone Americans call Americanism.
>
> Verily, with all the energy of my soul, I repudiate and I condemn all the opinions which the Apostolic Letter repudiates and condemns — all those false and dangerous opinions

to which, as the letter points out, certain persons have given the name of "Americanism." The whole episcopate of the United States, in their own name and in the name of their flocks, are ready to repudiate and condemn these errors. We cannot but be indignant that such a wrong should have been done us as to designate, as some have come to do, by the word "Americanism" errors and extravagances of this sort.

So, the "phantom heresy" was laid to rest, Father Hecker's name was cleared, and the Paulist Fathers were able to continue their work.

———

What was, and what is, the work of the Paulist Fathers? It is nothing less than the conversion of the United States to Catholicism. This is the purpose for which Father Hecker founded the congregation in 1858. This purpose was based on the extreme patriotism of Father Hecker. He so loved the United States that he wanted to give to all its citizens the most precious gift he could — the gift of the Catholic Faith that Hecker himself had found after a great deal of searching.

The Congregation of the Missionary Priests of St. Paul the Apostle (the Paulists) is the only religious community founded solely with the purpose of providing missionary work to the United States. It is strictly an American congregation, founded in America, by Americans, for Americans, and on American principles. The community would be conducted, said Father Hecker, "on American principles. The door opens both ways. No man stays with us longer than he chooses." Hence there were to be no vows, only a voluntary agreement to live the life of a Paulist.

Here is Father Hecker's definition of a Paulist:

He is a Christian man who aims at a Christian perfection consistent with his natural characteristics and the type of civilization of his country. A Paulist is to emphasize individuality; that is, to make individual liberty an essential element in every judgment that touches the life and welfare of the community and that of its members ... The individuality of a man cannot be too strong or his liberty too great when he is guided by the Spirit of God.

Father Hecker firmly believed that no country in the world was as ripe for conversion to Catholicism as the United States was, and this was because of the freedom and liberty enjoyed by her citizens. He believed that it should be possible to show them that the Catholic Faith is in accord with the principles of free liberty as expressed in the Declaration of Independence and the Constitution.

The basis of the work of the Paulists was to be missions; parish work would be subordinated to this. He said, "Our vocation is apostolic, conversion of souls to the Faith, of sinners to repentance, giving missions, defense of the Christian religion by conferences, lectures, sermons, the pen, the press, and the like works."

———

Forming this truly American congregation was no easy, or peaceful, task. In fact, if Father Hecker hadn't been expelled from the Redemptorist Order because of alleged insubordination, he would never have founded the Paulists.

Isaac Thomas Hecker was born on December 18, 1819, the youngest of five children of John and Caroline Freund Hecker, both of whom were born in Prussia. John professed no religious faith, while Caroline, though born Lutheran, professed the Methodist religion. Isaac grew up to have a deep yearning for a faith that would satisfy his intellectual curiosity.

Around the year 1841, Hecker met Orestes A. Brownson, a vigorous and powerful lecturer, social reformer, and editor of *The Boston Quarterly Review*. Brownson was also searching for religious truth. Years later Hecker was to remark, "Of all the men I ever knew,

Brownson had the most influence on me." From Brownson, Hecker became interested in social reform, particularly for the downtrodden laborer of those days.

In January of 1842, Hecker went to live at Brook Farm, a community started by George Ripley, later literary editor of the *New York Tribune*. The community was dedicated to a search for a better way of life. At this farm, where everybody labored in the fields, Hecker found the opportunity to converse with some of the intellectual giants of that era, for the men and women who lived at Brook Farm were of such caliber that Harvard College sent students there to be tutored. Such men as Nathaniel Hawthorne, George Bradford, Charles Dane, John Dwight, Ralph Waldo Emerson, and Henry Thoreau took part in discussions there. However, Hecker was unable to find in this man-made Utopia what he was looking for.

By this time Orestes Brownson was preaching and writing Catholic doctrine, although he himself had not yet received the gift of faith. Hecker too studied the Catholic religion and at length decided that he should enter the Church. He was conditionally baptized in old St. Patrick Cathedral by Bishop John McCloskey (later to become America's first cardinal) on August 2, 1844. Brownson was baptized less than a year later.

After his baptism, Hecker returned home to help his brothers in their bakery business. However, he felt the pull to the religious life, and, when he learned that several novices were sailing for the Redemptorist novitiate in Belgium, he decided to go with them and join the Redemptorist Order.

Hecker was almost 26 when he arrived in St. Trond, Belgium, in September of 1845 to begin his novitiate. Thirteen months later he took his vows and became a member of the Congregation of the Most Holy Redeemer. He was ordained a priest in London, England, on October 23, 1849. After serving as a parish priest for a year in England, he returned to New York on March 19, 1851, as one of a band of missionaries assigned to work in the United States.

The missionaries began to conduct missions in New York City and later went from town to town — Philadelphia, Youngstown,

Detroit, Wheeling, Louisville, Cincinnati, Albany, Richmond, Baltimore, New Orleans. At the mission in New Orleans, a young man by the name of James Gibbons listened attentively and shortly afterward decided he had a vocation to the priesthood.

Although not a great orator when the mission band began its missions, Father Hecker soon developed into a fluent, forceful, and effective speaker. His tall figure, pale blue eyes, and ruddy brown hair made him an impressive figure as he stood on a platform on which was erected a ten-foot cross over which a swath of white muslin was draped. It was said that no man could surpass him as a doctrinal and moral instructor, though he didn't attempt the emotional type of oratory.

—·—

At this time, German was the language spoken in all Redemptorist houses. The Americans among the Redemptorist mission band, however, were not comfortable with the arrangement. They felt it would be wise to establish a new house either in New York or in Newark, New Jersey, that could serve as headquarters for the English-speaking Redemptorists. Both Bishop James Bayley of Newark and Archbishop John Hughes of New York had made application for such a house. So, in May of 1857 the Redemptorists in New York wrote to the rector major of the order, a Father Mauron, presenting the plan to him.

Father Mauron's reply was disappointing. He opposed any separation within the congregation. Again, Father Walworth, the superior of the English-speaking group, wrote to the rector major explaining that English was the language of America and that the work of the missions was being damaged by the fact that Americans considered the Redemptorists established only for the German-speaking Catholics. "The fact that we have no English house is taken as proof that the congregation is essentially for Germans," he said.

By now it was generally felt that one of the Americans would have to go to Rome to present the whole matter to the rector major in person. Father Hecker was chosen, and he sailed for Rome on August 5, 1857, arriving on August 26. The rector major knew that he was coming because a letter had been sent to him by the provincial of the Redemptorists in New York explaining the purpose of the journey. Father Mauron therefore received Hecker politely and asked him to put down on paper his reasons for feeling that he had a right to make the trip.

On August 30, there was a meeting of the general council of the congregation, and Hecker was called to the meeting. Expecting to present his case to the council, Hecker was stunned when the rector major declared that it had been decided not to hear him. Furthermore, he was told that his coming to Rome constituted an act of disobedience that *ipso facto* dismissed him from the congregation — he was released from his vows and dismissed.

Hecker pleaded that he be given a hearing and a chance to defend himself and to show that his coming to Rome was important to the congregation, but the council refused. The constitution of the order forbade a member to go to Rome to place a matter before the general without permission, and the rector major said that he would feel derelict in his duty if he did not strictly enforce this rule.

———

Father Hecker decided to remain in Rome and appeal his case directly to the Holy See. He managed to win the sympathy of Cardinal Barnabo, prefect of the Propaganda, partly, at least, because of some letters he fortunately had from Archbishop Hughes, Bishop Bayley, and other American priests in good standing with the Vatican. Archbishop Hughes' letter stated that Hecker's missions had been the cause of bringing many converts to the Church and many lukewarm Catholics back to their religion, and recommended him as a "laborious, edifying, zealous, and truly apostolic priest."

Cardinal Barnabo met with the Redemptorists' rector major to try to get him to change his mind about Hecker's dismissal, but to no avail. The cardinal then suggested that Hecker ask Archbishop

Bedini, the secretary of the Propaganda, to present the entire matter to the pope. Bedini, who "had become as ardent a partisan of the American as was the cardinal," did so. Hecker, too, wrote a memorial to the pope asking that a special commission be appointed to examine and decide the affair.

Since this would take a while, Hecker then, again at the suggestion of Cardinal Barnabo, thought he might help his cause by writing articles for *Civilta Cattolica*, a leading Catholic journal in Rome. He wrote two articles showing the brighter side of the American character and the advantages of the American form of government. Then, to ensure as wide a circulation as possible for his views, he had reprints of the articles run off in pamphlet form and sent to the leading Catholic journals in Germany, France, Belgium, and England.

These two articles, probably better than anything else he wrote, show Hecker's thoughts about the Church in the United States and show how devoted he really was to his country. He wrote that the principles of government in the United States were decidedly in favor of the interest and success of the Catholic religion. He suggested that Divine Providence had prepared the American people for conversion and that all that remained was to take advantage of the situation.

In his first article, he outlined at some length the history of religion in the United States, particularly in New England. He discussed New England's early Calvinists, who believed in total depravity of the human being and a doctrine of eternal reprobation and eternal selection. In 1842, Hecker said, William Ellery Channing took a stand against these doctrines, and the result was Unitarianism, which taught the direct opposite of Calvinism. But many of the Unitarians were not satisfied with this system of belief either and again began searching for a new faith. In this search, however, they didn't approach the Catholic Church simply because they had been taught for a long time that the Catholic Church was false.

Hecker then discussed the groups that began to form to bring about a workable religion — Brook Farm and Fruitlands, both of which he was familiar with from firsthand knowledge. He pointed out that the people in these groups were really seeking the Catholic Church without realizing it. Fruitlands, for example, tried to prove that only a personal reform could correct the evils of life and that these evils were more personal than social or political.

He concluded his first article by declaring that an abundant harvest was ready in America because many people with "an unsatisfied active intelligence and an active mind" were ready to receive the truths of the Catholic religion.

The second article in *Civilta Cattolica* dealt with the character of political institutions in the United States and their effects on the religious development of the nation. Hecker quoted the "no establishment" clause of the Constitution that leaves all religious matters to Church rather than to State and forbids the State to interfere with religious beliefs. Therefore, Hecker wrote, the government of the United States and its natural advantages offer a wide door to the Catholic religion, a thesis that Cardinal Gibbons was to expound on years later.

Hecker wrote that it was necessary only to appeal to the intelligence of many outside the Church to convince them of the truth. He said that this would be a new campaign for the Church because in the Roman Empire the Church battled paganism and a declining civilization; in Western Europe the struggle was with barbarism, but in the United States it would be a campaign with an already civilized people and a young and energetic nation. He predicted that some day the Catholic Church might even look for missionaries from the United States to convert the Japanese and the Chinese.

These articles, as American as can be, were widely read and received no objections from any quarter. Among the readers was Pope Pius IX himself, who by now had taken a personal interest in Father Hecker's case.

Father Hecker had his first audience with the pope on December 17, 1857. After greeting each other, the pope asked, "And now, my son, what is your desire?"

"It is that Your Holiness would have the goodness to examine especially the purpose of my coming to Rome, since I regard the conversion of the American people as a work that the most intelligent and pious Catholics have at heart."

The pope replied that the matter was then being examined and that he would give his decision after receiving the report. He then continued, "The American people are engrossed in worldly things and in the pursuit of wealth, I am told."

"The United States, Your Holiness, is in its youth," Hecker replied, "and is like a young father of a family who is occupied in furnishing his house, and so busy with his own affairs. But the American people do not make money to hoard it, nor are they miserly."

"But in the United States there exists a too-unrestricted freedom," the pope went on. "All the refugees and revolutionaries gather there and are in full liberty."

"That is true, but this has its good side, too," Hecker replied. "Many of these, seeing that in the United States the Church is self-subsistent, and not necessarily connected with what they call despotism, begin to regard it as a divine institution and return to her fold."

The pope nodded: "Yes, the Church is as much at home in a republic as in a monarchy or in an autocracy."

Finally, on March 6, 1858, a decision was reached. The pope dispensed Hecker and his four American companions from their vows as Redemptorists and authorized them to form a new congregation devoted to missionary work in the United States under the direction of the hierarchy. After an audience with the pope during which he thanked him for the decision, Hecker returned to the United States. He had been gone for seven months.

The ex-Redemptorists immediately set to work organizing their new group. The rule for the new community was submitted to Archbishop Hughes and approved by him on July 7, 1858. Thus was born the most distinctively American community in the Catholic Church.

Father Hecker lived for thirty years after the founding of the Paulists, and he devoted himself during that time to building up his community and finding new methods for explaining the Catholic Church to Americans. He recognized the power of the printed word and in 1865 founded *The Catholic World*, a monthly magazine that served the Church well for more than a century.

In 1865, Hecker began the Catholic Publication Society to publish pamphlets and books. This exists today as the Paulist Press, one of the largest Catholic publishers in the United States.

In 1870, Baltimore's Archbishop Martin Spalding selected Hecker to attend the First Vatican Council as the archbishop's theologian. At this council, Hecker met two American bishops who were to be decisively affected by him — Bishop James Gibbons of North Carolina and Bishop John Ireland of St. Paul, Minnesota.

While in Rome, Hecker renewed acquaintances with those who had aided him thirteen years earlier after he had been dismissed from the Redemptorists. He also had two private audiences with the pope and returned to the United States buoyed up in spirit. He wrote:

> I return with new hope and fresher energy for that better future for the Church and humanity which is in store for both in the United States. This is the conviction of all intelligent and hopeful minds in Europe. They look to the other side of the Atlantic not only with great interest, but to catch the light which will solve the problems of Europe ... I return to my country a better Catholic and more an American than ever.

When he returned to the United States, Hecker was anxious to resume his work. In 1871, he tried to start a Catholic daily newspaper when he heard that a New York newspaper was for sale. However, he had to abandon this project when he suddenly became ill.

His health began to fail, and he suffered from nervous exhaustion and fatigue. In the summer of 1872, he suffered a complete nervous breakdown. He was in ill health the rest of his life and practically an invalid for his last five years. Nevertheless, he continued his writing in *The Catholic World*, and in 1887 a collection of his more important essays was published in a book, *The Church and the Age*.

One of the articles printed in the book was written on the occasion of Cardinal Gibbons being made a cardinal — and speaking in Rome in praise of the United States, particularly the principle of the separation of Church and State. (The episode opens the chapter about Cardinal Gibbons.) Hecker was lavish in his praise of Gibbons and showed himself in complete agreement with the cardinal's thinking when he wrote:

> The convictions he (Gibbons) has expressed have undoubtedly animated his whole life as a Catholic and a citizen, and all his countrymen will rejoice that he has uttered them with so much emphasis and bravery and that he has done it in the center of Christendom. Americans will thank him for it and account him as their representative, for he is fitted by his thoroughgoing spirit to interpret us to the people and the powers of the Old World. Americans do not want the pope, at the head of the most august assembly in the world, representing the whole Christian world, to speak in favor of empires, monarchies, or republics. That we do not want. What we want is the American cardinal to do what he has done, to have the courage of his convictions there and everywhere, as becomes our cardinal, so far as he represents the American republic.

Father Hecker loved the American character and thoroughly understood it. He was convinced that America had a future providential mission among the nations of the earth and that Catholicism was ideally suited to the personality of America. He wrote that

Europe, "under the lead of the religious revolution of the sixteenth century, turned its back on Catholicity and entered upon the downward road that ends in death; the republic of the United States, in affirming man's natural rights, started in the eighteenth century with its face to Catholicity and is in the ascending way of life to God."

He further wrote:

> When the nature of the American republic is better understood, and the exposition of Christianity is shaped in the light of its universal principles so as to suit the peculiarities of the American mind, the Catholic Church will not only keep her baptized American children in her fold, but will at the same time remove the prejudices existing in the minds of a large class of non-Catholics, and the dangers apprehended from the influence of republicanism will be turned into fresh evidence of the Church's divine character.

Archbishop Ireland perhaps best summed up Father Hecker's life and philosophy when he paid him this impressive tribute:

> Hecker looked on America as the fairest conquest for divine truth, and he girded himself with arms shaped and tempered to the American pattern. I think that it may be said that the American current, so plain for the last quarter of a century in the flow of Catholic affairs, is, largely at least, to be traced back to Father Hecker and his early co-workers. It used to be said of them in reproach that they were the "Yankee" Catholic Church; the reproach was their praise.
>
> His favorite topic in book and lecture was that the Constitution of the United States requires, as its necessary basis, the truths of Catholic teaching regarding man's natural state, as opposed to the errors of Luther and Calvin. The Republic, he taught, presupposes the Church's doctrine, and the Church ought to love a polity which is the offspring of her own spirit.

Archbishop John F. Noll

We have the best government under the best Constitution in the world.

— *ARCHBISHOP JOHN F. NOLL*

CHAPTER 7

Archbishop John F. Noll

B y the end of World War I, there was no doubt that the United States had finally matured as a nation. It had survived the struggling years of her adolescence and arrived on the world scene as one of the most powerful of nations.

Similarly, the Catholic Church in the United States also reached maturity by the end of World War I. Under Cardinal Gibbons, with the important aid of Archbishop Ireland, the Catholic Church was recognized as a powerful body wielding considerably more influence upon the country's leaders than at any other time.

However, the fact that both our nation and the Catholic Church in the United States reached maturity together does not mean that there were no more fights to be had. It simply meant that they must face their fights in a new role, as world leaders. As a matter of fact, the three decades from 1920 to 1950, when Archbishop John F. Noll was doing his most important work, presented perhaps greater challenges to the Church and the country than any other period of their history together. By and large, the Church and the country faced the problems together.

The most serious problems during those three decades were the Great Depression, the rise of Fascism in Italy and Germany, the spread of Communism under Josef Stalin, World War II, and the Cold War that continued almost to the end of the twentieth century. Catholic leaders, including Archbishop Noll, were as active as any Americans in combating these problems.

In the 1930s, Americans did not consider Communism to be the danger and the threat they later recognized it to be. Communism was an avowed enemy of Fascism, particularly the Fascism of Germany under Hitler and Italy under Mussolini. During the civil war in Spain, the Communists actually succeeded in brainwashing millions of Americans into believing that the fight was a case of democracy versus Fascism and that the Spanish Loyalists were democratic.

Bishop John Francis Noll's voice was one of the few that tried to show the complete fallacy of such belief. He was at least ten years ahead of many supposedly knowledgeable people in the United States when it came to recognizing the evils of Communism and the dangers of the Soviet state. Bishop Noll wrote often and vigorously against the spread of Communism during the 1930s, especially through his publication, *Our Sunday Visitor*, but also through his other writings.

In his book *It Is Happening Here*, he tried to show that Communism was "an imminent threat to our democracy, to our institutions, to our civil and religious liberties, to our inalienable rights." The bishop began the book with this statement:

> We have the best government under the best Constitution in the world. Let us preserve them in their present form by combating every un-American influence in our midst, and especially that which, based on pure materialism, is calculated to rob our nation of its attachment to religious and spiritual values, of its faith in God and trust in man.

It Is Happening Here presented documented evidence that literally millions of Americans, without realizing it, were actually promoting Communism through various organizations and associations. Bishop Noll demonstrated how Communism had managed to infiltrate such organizations as the American League Against War and Fascism, the American Civil Liberties Union, the Farmer Labor Party, and the American Federation of Teachers, as well as many of the country's labor unions and even many Protestant church groups.

During the Spanish Civil War, an organization calling itself American Friends of Spanish Democracy actively campaigned for funds to aid the Loyalist cause. This Communist organization managed to convince many good Americans that the Loyalists were fighting for democracy. Bishop Noll wrote article after article, pointing out the true identity of the Loyalists and showing why, if there must be civil war in Spain, our sympathy should be with the rebels.

Bishop Noll's words, however, did not reach enough people, or they were not convincing enough, for one of the great triumphs of Communism in this country was that the Communists were able to convince so many people of the righteousness of the Loyalists. The realization that Noll was right was acknowledged by thoughtful men only years later.

Yet even in the 1930s, when his voice was one of a minority of American patriots, Bishop Noll tried to point out the absurdity that Communism could be trying to bring democracy to Spain — or to anywhere else for that matter. He wrote:

> On serious thought, it must be clear to anyone that Communism and democracy are opposites. Under a democracy people have something themselves to say about the government, while under Communism there is absolutely no choice. There is one party, and that is the party in control, whether by silent or bloody revolutions. The dictatorship is one not *of* the proletariat, but one *over* the proletariat.

Bishop Noll never ceased his fight against Communism, especially during World War II, when Russia was our ally in the fight against Germany and Italy. At times, Bishop Noll became quite unpopular during the war, when the "official line" was that Communist Russia was our friend. The bishop saw through this role Russia was playing, and he never stopped urging his countrymen to recognize the danger to the world of Communist Russia. He was in the forefront of those few patriots who promoted a foreign policy of permitting Germany and Russia to destroy each other during the war rather than to permit the United States to aid Russia — and thus build her up — to the future detriment of the United States.

Bishop Noll was, naturally, vehemently opposed to Fascism, too, but he recognized Communism as a greater evil. He wrote that there are several differences between Communism and Fascism, among them these:

(1) Communism opposes the private ownership of property; Fascism does not.
(2) Fascism is not necessarily opposed to religion, while Communism is.
(3) Fascism is not the same in every country, while Communism is.
(4) As we know it, there is more freedom under Fascism than under Communism.
(5) Fascism was born of a desire to overcome Communism.

———

Archbishop Noll was best known for his work as founding editor of *Our Sunday Visitor*. He founded the publication in 1912 while he was still Father Noll and pastor of a parish in Huntington, Indiana. He edited the paper, and wrote at least two articles in every issue until illness forced him to stop a year before his death in 1956. Under his guidance, *Our Sunday Visitor* grew to become one of the most widely circulated Catholic newspapers in the world. It was mainly through *Our Sunday Visitor* and his numerous books and pamphlets (more than one hundred fifty pamphlets and fourteen books) that Archbishop Noll exercised his influence.

The founding of *Our Sunday Visitor* itself is testimony to Noll's patriotism and love of his Church, because he founded *Our Sunday Visitor* to combat Socialism and anti-Catholicism. Between 1909 and 1912, the Socialist movement in the United States grew so rapidly that one of its publications, *The Appeal to Reason*, had a circulation of more than a million a week. Other Socialist papers and magazines

were *The People's Press, The American Socialist, The Christian Socialist,* and *Melting Pot.* The Socialist Party itself and the Socialist Labor
Party had a following of several million people and constituted a formidable threat to the American way of life. This type of Socialism
was actually Communism and advertised and recommended the
writings of Marx, Hegel, and Engels.

The Appeal to Reason circulated chiefly among the laboring class.
Soon this publication received numerous protests against its atheistic character by Catholics who, of course, were part of the laboring
class. The party leaders, therefore, decided to split their propaganda.
They reserved *The Appeal* for preaching the wonderful advantages
of the Socialist way of life. Then they started a new publication
called *The Menace* to propagandize against God and religion in general — and the Catholic Church in particular.

Gradually, *The Menace* became the leader of the two publications,
as it reached the million mark in circulation, while *The Appeal* was
left to languish. Since anti-Catholicism was apparently so successful as a moneymaking venture for *The Menace,* soon no less than
thirty other publications became its imitators. The country was
lashed by bigotry more than ever before in its history. Some of the
picturesque titles of these anti-Catholic publications included *The
Peril, The American Defender, The American Sentinel, The Beacon Light,
The Crescent, The Converted Catholic Evangelist, The Crusader, The
Emancipator, The Guardian, The Good Citizen, The Jeffersonian, The
Liberator, The Masses, The Patriot, The Silverton Journal, The Sentinel
of Liberty, The Torch, Watson's Magazine,* and *The Yellow Jacket.*

Besides these anti-Catholic publications, there were also preachers who were sent around the country. They spoke to Socialist
groups and various Protestant organizations to defame the Catholic
Church — and always, of course, took up a collection and sold sub-
scriptions to the anti-Catholic periodicals.

Father Noll decided it was vital to destroy *The Menace* and its
imitators. Early in 1912, he had a printer reproduce two pages of
The Menace and on their reverse side print a proposed Catholic
answer in newspaper format. He mailed these samples to practically

every Catholic pastor in the United States. With them he sent a letter asking the pastors if they would patronize a Catholic newspaper of equal size that would refute the false accusations of the anti-Catholic publications.

The response of the pastors was enthusiastic, so on May 5, 1912 Father Noll published his first issue of *Our Sunday Visitor* with a press run of thirty-five thousand copies. By the end of the first year, the circulation was two hundred thousand, and it doubled itself by the end of the second year. After that the circulation rose at a slower rate until it reached a circulation of more than nine hundred sixty thousand, with many issues in excess of one million. All of this from a small beginning in an Indiana town with a population of less than fifteen thousand, by the pastor of a local parish.

———

John Francis Noll was born in Fort Wayne, Indiana, in 1875, the sixth child of John George and Anna Ford Noll; his ancestry was half-German and half-Irish. Anna died when the future archbishop was less than four years old, and less than six months after the birth of her next child, Loretto (the grandmother of this book's author). Later, John George married again, and his second wife, Mary McCleary, was to care for John Francis with great love. She had no time to spoil him, though, because Mary was to present her husband with twelve more children, so John Francis grew up with eighteen brothers and sisters.

The young John Noll always felt that he had a vocation to the priesthood, and he entered the Preparatory Seminary at St. Lawrence College, Mount Calvary, Wisconsin, in 1888. He received his philosophy and theology training at Mount St. Mary's of the West, in Cincinnati, Ohio, and was ordained on June 4, 1898.

Father Noll's first assignment as a priest was to Elkhart, Indiana. He was then sent to Logansport, Indiana, where he was an assistant pastor. His first pastorate was at Ligonier, where he had four other small towns as mission parishes. Later, he was transferred to

Besancon, then to Hartford City, and finally, in 1910, to St. Mary's Parish in Huntington.

By this time, Father Noll had already gained a reputation as a vigorous opponent of anti-Catholic lecturers. He would attend the lectures, making sure beforehand that he knew the personal history of the lecturer. Then, after the lecturer had had his say, Father Noll would jump to his feet, identify himself, and with his booming voice, supported by his large frame, begin to ask questions. He always managed to completely discredit the speaker, after which he would preach for a while about the true teachings of the Catholic Church. He would end by inviting his listeners to his own lectures about the teachings of the Church.

Father Noll first became a periodical publisher in 1908 while he was a pastor in Hartford City. Concerned that his parishioners were not receiving the Catholic instruction that he felt was so important, he began to think about a monthly magazine for them. The best thing of this sort that existed at that time was a thirty-two page monthly Catholic magazine called *Truth*, edited by Father Thomas Price, then a chaplain at an orphanage in Raleigh, North Carolina. (This same Father Price later met Father James Anthony Walsh of Boston, and together they founded the Catholic Foreign Mission Society of America, better known as Maryknoll. More information about Father Price is included in the chapter about additional patriotic Catholic churchmen of the United States.)

When his bundle of *Truth* arrived each month, Father Noll would take off the cover and substitute one of his own, calling the magazine *The Parish Monthly*. In addition to the regular contents of the magazine, he stitched in four or eight pages of local parish notes. When he explained to Father Price that this was how he was using the magazine, Father Price recommended to other clergy that the idea be taken up more generally.

After a while, though, Father Noll discovered that he had a talent for writing, and he could easily write the thirty-two pages of the magazine himself. When he did so, some of the neighboring pastors asked for copies of the magazine for their own parishes. Soon, more than two hundred parishes were ordering the magazine and defraying expenses by selling advertising to local merchants.

In 1910, when Father Noll was transferred to Huntington, Indiana, he took *The Parish Monthly* with him. He then had to find a printer at his new location. It happened that one of the two newspapers in Huntington bought the other one, and an entire printing plant was available. Father Noll bought the plant, with borrowed money, and then had more than enough equipment to produce his monthly magazine. When the provocation of *The Menace* made him decide to combat it, he had a fully equipped printing plant ready to produce *Our Sunday Visitor*.

Father Noll's original purpose for founding *Our Sunday Visitor* (to kill the socialistic and anti-Catholic publication, *The Menace*) was successful. After having financial problems, *The Menace* finally died, and, in 1919, the plant that had published it burned down. The plant's insurance company refused to honor the insurance claim because it believed the owners had started the fire.

—·—

Father Noll also founded *The Acolyte* in 1925. It was renamed *The Priest* in 1945 and is still being published today.

In addition to his periodicals, Father Noll was also the author of many best-selling books and pamphlets on almost every religious subject imaginable in his day. His book *Father Smith Instructs Jackson* was reprinted more than eighty times and reached more people than any other Catholic book except Cardinal Gibbons' *Faith of Our Fathers*. It was used by thousands of converts to Catholicism in their instruction courses. His other books included *Catholic Facts*, statistical facts about the Catholic Church throughout the world; *Civilization's Builder and Protector*, which gives the testimony of one hundred non-Catholic scholars and historians that the Catholic Church has throughout its history been the builder and protector of Christian civilization; *The Fairest Argument*, a five-hundred page book in which the bishop used only non-Catholic statements to defend the entire Catholic system of doctrine and practice; *It Is Happening Here*, which was discussed above; *The Decline of Nations*, which authenticates the gradual deterioration of morals, public and private, and the weakening of the Faith during the previous fifty years; *Our National Enemy Number One*, dealing with criticism by non-Catholics of the American public school system for eliminating religious instruction from the curriculum; *A Catechism on Birth Control; Catechism on Lewd Literature;* the *History of the Diocese of Fort Wayne;* and four volumes entitled *Religion and Life* for use in Catholic high schools as a textbook.

———

The biography of Bishop Noll is necessarily the story of the Church in the United States in the past fifty years. There are some few rare individuals whose lives are so intertwined with the events in their arena of living that they epitomize in themselves whole phases of the history of their times. Bishop Noll is one of those individuals.

The late Cardinal Samuel Stritch, Archbishop of Chicago, spoke the words quoted above on June 30, 1950, at the celebration of Bishop Noll's silver jubilee as a bishop. From the time of his consecration as the bishop of Fort Wayne in 1925, he was one of the leaders of the Catholic Church in the United States. Again quoting Cardinal Stritch: "Even a cursory glance at his record makes us wonder how one man, even a great, good man, could have done so many things for the Church. The answer is clear; Bishop Noll has one passion, one vehement passion, one almost boundless passion, and that is his love for the Church."

Every fall, the bishops of the United States meet in Washington, D.C. In 1925, no sooner had the new bishop of Fort Wayne entered the meeting room than Cardinal William O'Connell of Boston called him to the rostrum to serve as secretary. He was kept as secretary for several years.

At that same meeting in 1925, Bishop Noll was elected treasurer of the American Board of Catholic Missions, a position he retained until his death. He always had great interest in the missions. He served on the board of governors of the Catholic Church Extension Society, was one of the first to aid Maryknoll, and, through *Our Sunday Visitor*, had been supporting ten schools for Mexicans in the Archdiocese of San Antonio, all before the American Board of Catholic Missions was founded in 1924. In addition, earlier in 1925 he had built a motherhouse for the Missionary Catechists of Our Lady of Victory just outside of Huntington. The Missionary Sisters (as they began to be called in 1947) worked, and still work, among the Mexican children in the southwestern United States.

In 1927, Bishop Noll, having been a bishop for only two years, was elected to one of the seven top administrative posts of the National Catholic Welfare Conference, and he retained this position throughout most of his life. He was also episcopal chairman of Lay Organizations, comprising the National Council of Catholic Men, the National Council of Catholic Women, and the National Council of Catholic Nurses.

Bishop Noll was chosen to represent the American bishops at the International Catholic Week in Geneva, Switzerland, in 1930. At this meeting were assembled some of the greatest writers of the time — each to speak for the Catholics of his country. The audience to whom the speakers spoke was composed almost entirely of the delegates to the League of Nations. While in Geneva, the bishop made it a point to attend sessions of the League of Nations.

The other American bishops also appointed Bishop Noll as one of the original committee of four that formed the Legion of Decency in 1933. In 1937 he launched a drive against printed pornography that culminated in his selection as chairman of a committee that organized the National Organization for Decent Literature.

In 1943, Bishop Noll raised, through *Our Sunday Visitor*, one hundred fifty thousand dollars toward the erection of the façade of the National Catholic Welfare Conference building in Washington, D.C. The building served as an appropriate background for the statue "Christ, the Light of the World," which was also contributed by the readers of *Our Sunday Visitor*. The statue is a twenty-two foot bronze figure that was dedicated by the apostolic delegate in May of 1949. When the U.S. Conference of Catholic Bishops moved to new headquarters in Washington, the statue was also moved.

In 1946, Bishop Noll became the head of a committee of archbishops and bishops to raise five million dollars for the completion of the National Shrine of the Immaculate Conception in Washington, D.C. Unfortunately, he did not live to see the completion of the shrine. A bust of him is prominently displayed in the shrine, however, in a place of honor to commemorate his contributions toward the completion of the Shrine.

On September 2, 1953, Pope Pius XII raised Bishop Noll to the personal rank of archbishop. The honor was bestowed "in recognition of his long apologetic service to the Church through the press and as a pioneer among bishops who established and extended the National Catholic Welfare Conference in Washington." His work for the NCWC toward the conference's building was also noted, as was his chairmanship of the committee to raise funds to complete the National Shrine. Today there are plaques in both the U.S. Conference of Catholic Bishops building and in the National Shrine praising the work of Archbishop Noll.

The archbishop was also honored by the Catholic Press Association in 1953 with a special plaque for his "monumental contributions" to the Catholic press. He had been one of the founders of the Catholic Press Association in addition to his other work for the Catholic press.

———•———

In 1928, the Democratic Party nominated Alfred E. Smith, a Catholic, as its candidate for president of the United States — the first time a Catholic had ever been nominated for the highest office in the land. Thirty-two years later, in 1960, a Catholic would be elected president. Considerable anti-Catholic literature appeared in the campaign of 1960, but it was all mild in comparison with the violence with which anti-Catholicism burst on the scene before the 1928 election; this is testimony to the progress made by Catholic Church leaders between 1928 and 1960 in proving to their fellow countrymen that Catholics are loyal citizens.

During the 1928 presidential campaign, the Democratic Party simply wasn't prepared for the wave of anti-Catholicism that overtook the country. Smith quickly became "Alcoholic Smith" (because the repeal of prohibition was a plank in the Democratic platform) — "the craven minion of the pope, already preparing to take over the White House as an American Vatican." Herbert Hoover, on the other hand, although he didn't seek the role, was cast as "the White Knight of Americanism, loins girt and lance upraised to save the country from the black hell of Romanism."

John J. Raskob, chairman of the National Democratic Committee (and also a Catholic), chose Michael Williams, the editor of *The Commonweal*, to handle the religious angle of the campaign for Smith. Williams, in turn, went to the man he knew was best able to marshal the forces of truth in the fray — Bishop Noll.

Bishop Noll assembled a huge scrapbook of the anti-Catholic literature that suddenly flooded the country. He duplicated them by Photostat and distributed them to other members of the hierarchy, important priests, and various civil leaders. The literature was not hard to find because numerous publications appeared with the sole purpose of poisoning the minds of the American people against the Catholic Church. Some of the publications, such as *The American Freeman* and the Ku Klux Klan paper, *The Fellowship Forum*, had vast circulations and the backing of powerful organizations. Books and tracts appeared in bookstores — books like *Three Keys to Hell, or Rum, Romanism, and Ruin*; *House of Death and Gate of Hell*; and *The Pope and the War*.

Each week in *Our Sunday Visitor*, Bishop Noll took up the latest batch of accusations and patiently answered them point by point from the writings of historians and theologians. At the same time he was careful not to urge his readers to vote for Smith or to impugn the Republican Party in any way. As a matter of fact, the entire Catholic Church in the United States was careful in this respect. No cardinal, archbishop, or bishop endorsed Smith. The annual bishops' meeting, usually held in October, was purposely postponed until mid-November so nobody would suspect that the bishops met to discuss politics. The convention of the National Council of Catholic Men was also postponed for the same reason, and when the Knights of Columbus met in August, the chairman opened the proceedings by declaring that "if any delegate should so much as mention the name of either candidate for the presidency, he will be declared out of order."

Although the Catholic Church bent over backwards to avoid politics, some of the Protestant churches did not. A Methodist bishop declared, "We have sent out one million pledge cards to southern Democrats to pledge themselves to vote and work against Smith, to contribute money, and organize anti-Smith clubs." And the National Lutheran Editors' Association, at a meeting in Columbus, Ohio, passed a resolution stating that "the peculiar allegiance that a faithful Catholic owes to the teachings of his Church, toward a foreign sovereign, who also claims supremacy in secular affairs, may clash with the best interests of the country."

When the National Lutheran Editors' Association made this statement, the general secretary of the National Catholic Welfare Conference asked Bishop Noll to issue a rebuttal. The bishop did so, basing the rebuttal entirely on the writings of Protestants. The Associated Press carried this rebuttal, and the editors of *The Atlantic Monthly* considered the issue so important that it published a debate on the subject.

An interesting aspect of the 1928 presidential election is that the critics of the Catholic Church and of Alfred E. Smith failed to consider the many prominent Catholics who were Republicans. Joseph Scott, a Catholic and a Knight of St. Gregory, delivered Herbert Hoover's nomination speech at the convention. Colonel P.H. Callahan of Louisville, one of Hoover's principal backers, had headed the Religious Prejudice Commission of the Knights of Columbus during and after World War I, and was also a papal knight. Senator Charles Curtis, who was Hoover's running mate on the Republican ticket, had been baptized a Catholic. And a Catholic priest, a close personal friend of Herbert Hoover, had officiated at Hoover's wedding.

Al Smith, "The Happy Warrior" as Franklin D. Roosevelt had called him, went down in what has been called "the most glorious defeat ever experienced by a presidential candidate." However, Bishop Noll felt that this defeat did no lasting harm to the Catholic Church. In fact, it might have done some good because it brought bigotry out into the open and gave many fair-minded people an opportunity, for many of them the first such opportunity, to learn the truth about the teachings of the Catholic Church.

Ellery Sedgwick, editor of *The Atlantic Monthly*, was able to express his admiration for "the dignity, the forbearance, and the good citizenship of the Roman Catholic clergy in America." He continued:

> To the Americanism preached by Ireland and Gibbons is now added the Americanism practiced by Smith. The Catholic Church in America is in the civic sense an American church. Ultramontanism is in this country a lost cause. To the limbo where it belongs, Protestant bigotry must follow. The conduct of the Church, high above reproach in this bad crisis, will not be forgotten.

———

In the process of defending the Church against the forces of anti-Catholicism, Bishop Noll wrote often about the separation of Church and State. He, like Cardinal Gibbons and others before him, emphasized the difference between this separation in the United States and that practiced in some European countries:

> In the United States, not only is perfect freedom granted to all religions to carry on their work without interference

from the State, but the Church's religious activities are actively encouraged by the State. This sort of separation of Church and State has always been quite satisfactory to the Catholic Church, which demands only liberty to execute her divine mission. But in European countries separation of Church and State has almost invariably meant a great curtailment of religious activities after the confiscation of property of the Church and the closing of its schools.

When discussing this subject, the bishop always asked for the meaning of the words "separation of Church and State." "Do you understand it in the American sense of 'a free Church in a free State,' or in the European sense of 'an enslaved Church in an anti-religious State'?" He was, however, also quick to point out that the Catholic Church does not believe in absolute separation of Church and State:

> The Church's clear teaching is that there should be cooperation rather than antagonism between the State and Church because both deal with the same citizens, one in relation to his eternal interests and the other in relation to his temporal interests. Where practically all the people of a nation are also members of the one Church, under the democratic principle that the people rule, there certainly should not be a complete separation of Church and State, especially not such separation as enemies of the Church demand, which consists in the subjugation of the Church, divinely commissioned to promote religion and morality, to the State. Where is the recognition of people's inalienable rights to liberty or religious practice and the pursuit of eternal happiness under such conditions?

Bishop Noll also consistently pointed out that the problem of the union of Church and State was far more often found in Protestant countries than in Catholic countries. Such union in Protestant countries was also much closer than in Catholic countries, because in Protestant countries Church and State were usually united in the same individual. The head of the State was also head of the Church. Thus, he wrote, until World War I, Russia, Germany, England, Norway, and Sweden had such a union of Church and State.

Although he did not want a union of Church and State in the United States, Bishop Noll wrote and spoke vigorously against those who promoted the "separation of religious influence from the lives of the people and the nation." He felt strongly that America could be strong only when its citizens obeyed moral principles. "Genuine citizenship is based on justice," he wrote, "as is also a sound social and economic order, but there can be no justice without religion."

He also wrote, "Good citizenship presupposes the training of youth along the lines of virtue." This was what prompted him to campaign so vigorously in article after article in *Our Sunday Visitor* and in his book *Our National Enemy Number One* for returning God to the classroom. He wrote:

> What a wonderful opportunity America has had to foster the old-fashioned patriotism in the schools of the nation, and what little advantage has been taken of this opportunity! Since patriotism can best be built on a religious foundation, what a blunder has been made in keeping religion out of the school curriculum as something which is of no concern to the nation!

While defining "our national enemy number one" as "education without religion," Bishop Noll emphasized that he had not the slightest hostility toward public schools. He had no objections, he said, to what is taught in the public schools, but rather to "what is *not* taught in the schools." His criticism was of the "system completely divorced from the inspiration of religion" which, he said, is also "out of keeping with the beliefs of the majority of the people."

He emphasized that religious schools antedated the non-religious schools by many decades, so it was incorrect to say that non-religious schools were an American tradition. He pointed out that "Washington, Jefferson, Madison, Hamilton, and Lincoln never sat in a public school room; neither did Theodore nor Franklin Roo-

sevelt." He sincerely believed that there could be nothing unconstitutional about teaching the fundamentals of religion in the public schools. He felt that the Constitution, the Declaration of
Independence, and other American documents were themselves
based on religious principles, and that "the Constitution merely pro-
vides that no particular form of religion be recognized, no established church — which is an entirely different thing from an implied
endorsement of the atheistic policy now in vogue in the schools."

Bishop Noll also tried to make it clear that his advocacy of religious instruction in public schools was not recommended because
he thought this would help Catholics in some way, because "they will
continue to conduct their own schools." Rather, he felt this was
important to the country at large because he considered it imperative for good citizenship for children to know the fundamentals of
religion.

———•———

It was probably his fight against Communism, which he seemingly
waged alone for many years, that best shows Archbishop Noll's
intense patriotism. When Stalin and Hitler signed the Nazi-Soviet
Pact of August 1939, he thought that Communism would finally be
recognized for the evil that it was. He was able to write:

> Communism itself has not changed its face nor its aims
> and objectives, and what its great high priest has recently done
> to destroy the confidence of the world in its declared purposes,
> the writer has, for the past ten years, declared that it would
> likely do. The many who until recent months believed that we
> had taken Communism too seriously, and had unwarrantedly
> held that millions of Americans were unwittingly promoting
> its interest, are now telling us that they were wrong and that
> we were right.
>
> It is really interesting to behold men who could not be
> induced, even to save their face before the public, to denounce

Communism in the same breath with Fascism, now bitterly excoriating Stalin and all that he stands for.

The bishop had to frankly bemoan the fact that others in the United States who had control of the communications media did not show the patriotism he had. The morale of America at the beginning of World War II, he said, would have been one hundred percent higher if these people had "all cooperated in holding up the American form of government as the best ever devised, and if they had done all in their power to promote a brotherhood of love rather than to divide the citizenry into groups controlled by mutual animosities and hates."

Unfortunately, the bishop's confidence that most people would recognize the evils of Communism after the Nazi-Soviet Pact did not prove true. After Germany attacked Russia and the Soviet Union became our ally, Communism regained its good name. Yet, throughout the war, Bishop Noll never stopped writing against Communism. This was not the most popular thing to do, because the Soviet Union was supposed to be our friend, and our governments were cooperating in trying to defeat Germany. Nevertheless, Bishop Noll had the courage of his convictions, and, as history has shown, he was right.

He protested vehemently when Roosevelt, Stalin, and Churchill met to plan the future of Europe and the United States permitted Russia to take over the Eastern European countries that remained Soviet-dominated until the 1990s. He was particularly concerned about the betrayal of Poland into Communist hands because so many Americans of Polish ancestry had given their lives in the war against Germany and because the Catholic country was being delivered into the hands of the atheists. If Bishop Noll's warnings had been heeded, the United States would have avoided many of the problems it was faced with throughout the Cold War.

———

When Archbishop Noll died on July 31, 1956, at the age of eighty-one, tributes by the thousands poured into the offices of *Our Sunday Visitor*. Cardinal Francis Spellman of New York called him "outstanding as a citizen, as a priest, and as a bishop." Other tributes called him a leader in the Church in the United States who would be deeply missed.

Archbishop Fulton J. Sheen

We Catholics love America — we love it more than Italy, more than Germany, more than Russia. We love its Constitution and its traditions, and we want to see them preserved.

— *ARCHBISHOP FULTON J. SHEEN*

CHAPTER 8

Archbishop Fulton J. Sheen

By the middle of the twentieth century, the Catholic Church in the United States had come a long way from the days of suspicion it experienced only a half-century before. Perhaps a prime example of that occurred in 1958 when President Dwight D. Eisenhower convened a meeting to promote his administration's 3.9 billion dollar foreign aid program. Present at the meeting, in addition to President Eisenhower, were former President Harry Truman, Vice President Richard Nixon, Secretary of State John Foster Dulles, Secretary of Defense Neil H. McElroy, Adlai Stevenson, Thomas Dewey, and Dean Acheson. Some of the country's religious leaders were also invited, including the president of the National Council of Churches, the president of the Synagogue Council of America, and a representative of the Catholic Church.

The Catholic Church was represented at this meeting not by an American cardinal but by the most popular Catholic at the time — Bishop Fulton J. Sheen. Well before this meeting, Bishop Sheen had earned a reputation as one of the United States' great patriots. In 1955, for example, the senior class at the University of Notre Dame named him "Patriot of the Year" for its annual Washington's Birthday celebration. Perhaps this reputation for patriotism was one of the reasons for his invitation to speak at this meeting, but undoubtedly the main reason was Bishop Sheen's fame that resulted from his popular television program.

Naturally, Bishop Sheen supported President Eisenhower's program. He told the participants, "Our moral duty to aid others is because the earth and the fullness thereof were made by God for all the people of the earth, and not for the privileged advantage of a few." This would hardly be an unexpected position for the head of the Society for the Propagation of the Faith, the Catholic Church's principal mission organization, to take.

———

Nobody in the Catholic Church before or since has had the success on television that Bishop Sheen had from February 1952 until April 1957. Still today one often hears the expressed wish that we had another Bishop Sheen who could explain Catholic doctrine on television as he did.

Bishop Sheen won an Emmy in 1952 as "Most Outstanding Television Personality," quipping as he accepted his award, "I wish to thank my four writers, Matthew, Mark, Luke, and John." He made the covers of *Time*, *TV Guide*, and *Look* magazines. *Look* named his program the "Best Religious Program" for three years, *Radio and Television Daily* named him "Man of the Year" on television, and the Advertising Club of New York named him "Our Television Man of the Year." The *Time* cover story said that he was "perhaps the most famous preacher in the U.S., certainly America's best-known Roman Catholic priest, and the newest star of U.S. television."

When he was on opposite Milton Berle ("Mr. Television") on NBC and Frank Sinatra on CBS, Bishop Sheen had 5.5 million viewers a week. Sinatra's program was canceled, and Berle's went down ten rating points. Later, he was on opposite Groucho Marx. His office was receiving twenty-five thousand letters a day, many of them with money for the missions.

The name of his program was *Life Is Worth Living*. It was originally on the small Du Mont Network, which considered the program a public service broadcast. No one expected it to become as popular as it did. As it grew in popularity, the Admiral Corporation sponsored the show — the first time a corporation advertised its products on a religious program. In 1956 the show was being carried on 113 television stations and 300 radio stations, with an estimated audience of 30 million, and in 1957 it moved from Du Mont to ABC Television.

Bishop Sheen always appeared in his full episcopal regalia — a black cassock with purple piping, a purple cape, a purple skullcap, and a large gold pectoral cross on his chest. Although the programs were all in black and white in those early days of television, he still made an impressive appearance. Few people realized that the bishop was only five feet seven inches tall and weighed no more than 140 pounds.

Perhaps what most people remember were his piercing eyes as he looked directly into the camera. A theatrical and flamboyant showman, he knew how to mix serious matters with corny jokes, when to move upstage, when and how to modulate his voice, and the timing of a pause. Actors such as Loretta Young and comedians such as Jackie Gleason marveled at his sense of timing. An actor named Ramon Estevez was so impressed with him that, with the bishop's permission, he changed his name to Martin Sheen.

Bishop Sheen's only prop was a blackboard at the top of which he wrote "JMJ," which viewers soon learned stood for "Jesus, Mary, Joseph." (He wrote "JMJ" at the top of everything he wrote, a habit formed when he was in grammar school.) When the two-sided blackboard was out of camera range, a stagehand would turn it over. When the bishop moved back to a clean blackboard, he would smilingly inform his viewers that "my angel, Skippy," had cleaned the board for him. His blackboard became such a well-recognized prop that, in 1995, Liguori Publications published an anthology of some of his talks under the title *From the Angel's Blackboard*.

He always spoke without notes, but his material was so well organized that he always ended precisely on time. At the beginning, he simply asked his director to signal him when he had fifteen seconds to go, but later that was extended to two minutes. He ended his talks with a benediction and his most famous phrase, "God love you."

Bishop Sheen estimated that he spent thirty hours in preparation for each of his programs, preparing numerous outlines, but he insisted that he did not memorize the talks. He told one interviewer that being a good speaker "is ten percent delivery and ninety percent thinking, study, sweat, and hard work." Not only did he decide on the content and how he wanted to present it, but he also practiced each talk by giving it in both French and Italian. (He also could read Greek and German, in addition to being fluent in Latin.) This, he said, helped him to clarify the subject in his mind.

Although Bishop Sheen created a sensation when he began to appear on national television in 1952, he was already well-known as a great preacher in Catholic circles because he was a regular speaker on radio's *The Catholic Hour* from 1930 to 1952. Bishop John F. Noll published thirty-seven of then-Monsignor Sheen's radio addresses at Our Sunday Visitor during those twenty-two years, and millions of copies were distributed by the National Council of Catholic Men. One talk alone, *Queen of Seven Swords*, delivered in 1934, went through eleven editions by 1948. The programs were broadcast over NBC stations and then rebroadcast over a General Electric Company station that transmitted them worldwide.

He was also renowned for his writing. Besides the printed radio talks, over a period of fifty-four years he wrote sixty-six books, seven booklets, and fourteen pamphlets. He wrote two syndicated columns, one for the secular press that ran for thirty years and the other, called "God Loves You," for the Catholic press. He and his works seemed to be everywhere.

It was for these reasons that one of his biographers, Thomas C. Reeves, called Archbishop Sheen "the leading American Catholic of the twentieth century." He is not the only one to think that. The Internet *Catholic Daily* took a poll to see who people thought were the most important Catholics of the twentieth century. With 23,455 people casting ballots, Archbishop Sheen came in fourth place behind Pope John Paul II, Mother Teresa, and St. Padre Pio. Archbishop Sheen was the top American.

During most of this time, he was known as Monsignor Fulton J. Sheen. He was made a papal chamberlain (Very Reverend Monsignor) in 1934 and a domestic prelate (Right Reverend Monsignor) in 1935. He didn't become a bishop until 1951 when he was named an auxiliary bishop to Cardinal Francis J. Spellman of New York. He was given the title of archbishop in 1969 and named assistant at the Pontifical Throne in 1976.

———•———

The lives of John F. Noll and Fulton J. Sheen overlapped. Their viewpoints were identical, especially when it came to the political and social issues of the day, and they complemented each other with the work they did. While Bishop Noll was opposing Fascism and Communism in the pages of *Our Sunday Visitor* in the 1930s and 1940s, Monsignor Sheen was doing the same thing on *The Catholic Hour* on radio.

The efforts of the two great patriots merged when Bishop Noll's publishing company, Our Sunday Visitor, published Monsignor Sheen's radio addresses. One of Monsignor Sheen's addresses in 1938 was on patriotism. In 1939 he spoke on freedom twice, and Our Sunday Visitor published the talks under the titles *Freedom, Part One* and *Freedom, Part Two*.

The late '30s, of course, were the time when Adolf Hitler in Germany and Josef Stalin in the Soviet Union were spreading their ideologies of Fascism and Communism. After World War II began in Europe, Our Sunday Visitor published more of Monsignor Sheen's radio addresses: *Communism, Capitalism, and Property* in 1939; *Peace: The Fruit of Justice* in 1940; *War and Guilt* in 1941; *Freedom and Peace* in 1941; *Peace* in 1942; and *The Crisis in Christendom* in 1943.

Although he opposed Fascism, Monsignor Sheen recognized that Communism was far worse. During a private audience with Pope Pius XI, the pope advised the monsignor to study Communism and never to speak in public during his pontificate without revealing its fallacies. Monsignor Sheen took that advice to heart. Besides his *Catholic Hour* talks, he published five anti-Communist pamphlets during 1936 and 1937, and he spoke out against Communism every chance he got. During Lent in 1936, in a sermon delivered in St. Patrick's Cathedral, he said:

Why can't the modern mind see there is nothing new in Communism? It is the logical development of civilization which for the last four hundred years has been forgetting God. Communism is the new slavery that takes possession not only of the body, the labor, and the private property of man, but also of his soul.

He, perhaps, was never stronger in denouncing Communism than when he spoke at a rally in New York's Carnegie Hall. As reported in the December 10, 1938, issue of *The New York Times*, he said:

We were silent before when two million Kulaks met death and sixty thousand churches were closed by an atheistic government in Russia. We were silent before when twenty thousand churches and chapels were desecrated, burned and pillaged, and when six thousand diocesan clergy were murdered in Spain. We were silent before when eleven Mexican bishops were exiled and one hundred thirty-one churches in the state of Tobasco alone were taken down, stone by stone, and when Socialist education was made compulsory. But now the secret is out. Those who cannot pull God down from heaven are driving his creatures from the face of the earth.

That silence, he said, was about to end:

Now we shall let the broad stroke of our challenge ring out on the shields of the world's hypocrisy; now we shall with the sword of justice cut away the ties that bind down the energies of the world. Now we shall lift up our voices and say to all persecuting nations, "This is not the first of your persecutions, but it shall be the last."

As Monsignor Sheen continued to speak out against Fascism and Communism, some anti-Catholic organizations questioned whether Catholics could truly be patriotic. Didn't they owe sub-servience to the pope in Rome? He answered his critics in 1938 when he said:

> We Catholics love America — we love it more than Italy, more than Germany, more than Russia. We love its Consti-tution and its traditions, and we want to see them preserved; we love the flag which is the symbol of our liberty, and for that reason we reject a system which recognizes only one flag — namely, the red flag.

In 1940, with war raging in Europe but not yet in the United States, Monsignor Sheen published his book *Whence Comes War*. He answered those who asked why God didn't stop the war by replying that God could not do so without destroying human freedom — since man started the war, it was up to him to end it.

In that book, too, he wrote about the relationship between reli-gion and democracy:

> A religion can live without democracy; it can live under tyranny, persecution, and dictatorship — not comfortably, it is true, but heroically and divinely. But democracy will degen-erate into demagogy by selling itself to the highest bidder.

By "the highest bidder," he meant that the source of right and wrong was determined by public opinion polls. He said that democ-racy's survival "depends upon an electorate imbued with morality which God and religion alone can give."

Although at times Monsignor Sheen seemed to advocate war against Fascism and Communism, he actually was a bit of an isola-tionist before the United States was dragged into the war. When the University of Notre Dame gave him an honorary degree in 1941 and he delivered the baccalaureate sermon, he said that some things were not worth fighting for. He proceeded to list a number of things that he saw as the moral decay of America, including monopolistic capitalism, corrupt labor unions, godless education, a system that encourages the breakup of marriage through divorce, and a system of tolerance that "breeds atheism, anti-religion, and anti-Semitism."

He was making the point that it was not America as it was that should be saved, but the America as it ought to be — "a nation rededicated to God and to the basic principles of the Declaration of Independence." He continued to make that point throughout the 1940s. In 1948, he published the book *Communism and the Conscience of the West* in which he said that America was rotting from within and would pay the inevitable price of destruction unless it reformed.

———•———

The man who was to become Archbishop Fulton J. Sheen was born Peter John Fulton Sheen in the small town of El Paso, Illinois, on May 8, 1895, the eldest child of Newt and Delia Sheen. His family moved to Peoria when he was five. He dropped his name Peter when he was in the first grade at St. Mary's School in Peoria, and he was thereafter known as Fulton, his mother's maiden name.

Sheen was a bright and studious boy, definitely more devout than most school children. When he was confirmed at the age of twelve, he dedicated himself to the Blessed Virgin, to whom he continued a special devotion throughout his life. He also realized by that time that he had a vocation to the priesthood, an aspiration already accepted by his parents.

He attended Spalding Institute, a small, all-male Catholic high school in Peoria. When he was a sophomore, his family moved to a farm outside Peoria, and Sheen stayed with his uncle (Delia's brother). During summers he worked on his father's farm, a job he detested. At school he didn't try to play sports because of his small size; he weighed only about 115 pounds at the time. (Later in his life he took up tennis, which he played twice a week well into his 70s.) As valedictorian of his graduating class in 1913, he is reported to have delivered a memorable speech, an indication of things to come.

He attended St. Viator College, a small college (only twenty-five students when Sheen entered) in Bourbonnais, Illinois, run by the Viatorian Fathers. He joined the debate team and by his sophomore year was the star of the team. One of the team's victories was over the University of Notre Dame, a significant achievement for a small college.

St. Viator's campus magazine could have been describing Fulton Sheen much later in his life when it declared:

> No one has shed greater "sheen" upon the Class of 1917 than this golden-tongued, fiery, young Demosthenes, who has shown his quick wit, versatility, and power of mind so often on the debating platform. In stature he is rather abbreviated, slight of build, quick, business from the word go, with shining eyes that catch you and flood you with his striking personality.

Besides performing on the debate team, Sheen had his own column in the campus magazine and published twelve articles. Again a harbinger of things to come.

After graduation in 1917, Sheen headed for the seminary — St. Paul's Seminary in St. Paul, Minnesota. Archbishop John Ireland founded the seminary in 1894 to educate men throughout the Upper Midwest. Archbishop Ireland died a year after Sheen entered the seminary.

At the seminary, Sheen was immersed in neo-Thomism or neo-Scholasticism, the philosophy and theology of St. Thomas Aquinas. In 1907, Pope Pius X had made Thomism the only orthodox Catholic theology, and in 1917, the year Sheen entered the seminary, the revised Code of Canon Law mandated that all professors of philosophy and theology teach the doctrines and principles of Thomas Aquinas.

During his seminary days, Sheen began a practice that he continued for the rest of his life: a daily Holy Hour in the chapel before the Eucharist, usually early in the morning before Mass. (Among many people who later emulated him in this practice was Cardinal Joseph Bernardin of Chicago.)

Sheen was ordained a priest on September 19, 1919, at the age of twenty-four. He then continued his education at The Catholic University of America in Washington, D.C., where, a year later, he received both his Bachelor of Canon Law and Bachelor of Sacred Theology degrees. Then he was off to the University of Louvain in Belgium, where his classes were taught in French and Latin, to study for his Ph.D. It was his first visit to Europe, and he took advantage of vacations to see as much of it as he could — Rome (where he had his first audience with a pope), London, Paris, and other major cities. He also took a trip that traced the journeys of St. Paul.

When he received his Ph.D., with greatest distinction, in 1923, he was invited to continue his studies for a rare postdoctoral degree, called the *agrege*. It meant that he would be "aggregated" (eligible to join) the Louvain faculty. He was the first American to receive this invitation. While studying for that degree, though, he was not required to remain at Louvain, so he moved to Rome. There he studied at both the Angelicum and the Gregorium universities.

That year, too, he made his first visit to the Shrine of Our Lady of Lourdes. It was the first of about thirty visits there through the years.

Father Sheen received his *agrege* degree, with great distinction, in 1925. Soon after, Longmans-Green and Company published his first book, *God and Intelligence*, which had been his dissertation for the *agrege* degree. G. K. Chesterton wrote the introduction. Neither man knew that someday this young priest would be known as "the American Chesterton."

Father Sheen was thirty years old now, with extraordinary academic credentials. But he was also still a priest of the Diocese of Peoria, and Bishop Edmund Dunne called him back to the diocese and assigned him as a curate in one of the poorest parishes in Peoria. He threw himself into this assignment with great energy and was a model associate pastor. His sermons packed the church; he visited every home in the parish, and he was successful at winning converts and bringing people back to the Church.

He was there only eight months, however. For Bishop Dunne was quite aware that Father Sheen was destined for bigger things — two years earlier, he had promised Catholic University that the priest could join its faculty. In making the assignment to the poor parish, the bishop said, he was testing Father Sheen's obedience; he passed the test.

Father Sheen began his teaching assignment at The Catholic University of America in 1926. He remained there for twenty-four years. During most of that time he taught two courses a semester, two days a week. This allowed him time to write his books and to become a popular speaker on *The Catholic Hour*. He began to give powerful sermons in St. Patrick's Cathedral in New York, commuting by train from Washington to New York.

Father Sheen was made a monsignor in 1934. He always spent his summers abroad and traveled throughout the United States to keep speaking dates. *Time* magazine reported in 1940 that he filled one hundred fifty speaking engagements while teaching at Catholic University. All this, of course, prepared him well for his role as teacher and preacher on his television program.

———

Besides being known as a great preacher and teacher, Monsignor Sheen was renowned for the hundreds of people who converted to Catholicism as a result of his efforts. Among his most famous converts were Clare Boothe Luce, Henry Ford II, and the former Communists Louis Budenz and Bella Dodd. In his sermons and radio talks, he announced that he would give personal instruction to all who requested it, and many did request it.

By 1945, Monsignor Sheen was conducting regular classes for those interested in joining the Church. When he traveled from Washington to New York for his *Catholic Hour* radio programs, potential converts would gather at the Roosevelt Hotel, where he stayed. Women from his staff would greet them and play audiotapes that Monsignor Sheen had prepared. Then he would appear to answer questions and talk to each individual. He also conducted convert classes in his home in Washington, usually spending from forty to one hundred hours with each individual. He also gave them copies of his book *Preface to Religion*, which he wrote in 1946.

The stream of converts became so large that various anti-Catholic organizations took note of it. Chief among Monsignor Sheen's opponents were Paul Blanshard and an organization called Protestants and Others United for the Separation of Church and State. Of course, the Catholic Church had always favored the separation of Church and State because the Church could prosper best when not controlled by the State. But evangelical Christian leaders became alarmed when their parishioners began joining the Catholic Church.

Already by 1945, years before he started his television program, Monsignor Sheen was so prominent that he was often referred to as a top Catholic official. In that year, Harold Ockenga, speaking at a convention of the National Association of Evangelicals, said that the Catholic Church hierarchy was trying to control the U.S. government. He said, "The political activity of the Roman Catholic hierarchy is doubly dangerous because Americans are unaware that the philosophy of Monsignor Fulton J. Sheen may involve a change in American culture almost as fundamental as that of Josef Stalin."

Another attack was made by William Ward Ayer, a popular leader of the Baptist Church in New York. In two articles in the *United Evangelical Action*, he tried to indicate that Monsignor Sheen's converts (specifically, Ford, Luce, and Budenz) were really not true Protestants to begin with. Ayer attacked Monsignor Sheen's character and warned that the Catholic Church was "planning complete religious totalitarianism that will destroy our religious liberty."

Later, when the television program became such a success, the *Christian Beacon* called Bishop Sheen part of "a very real threat" to the United States from "aggressive papists." It showed that anti-Catholicism was still rife in the United States. Undoubtedly, though, Bishop Sheen helped tremendously to eliminate much of that antagonism.

———•———

In 1948, Cardinal Francis J. Spellman invited Monsignor Sheen to join him on a trip to Australia. Cardinal Spellman could easily rival Monsignor Sheen when it came to patriotism. He was a personal friend of President Franklin Roosevelt, whom he greatly admired. Besides being the Archbishop of New York, Spellman was also the nation's military vicar. During World War II he traveled throughout the world to visit American troops and offer Mass for them. In 1943, for example, he covered forty-six thousand miles in twenty-four weeks, and in 1944 his European tour lasted three months.

Cardinal Spellman thought of Monsignor Sheen as his protégé. In 1942, when he asked the Vatican for another bishop for the Military Ordinariate (now known as the Archdiocese for the Military Services) and recommended three candidates, he described Monsignor Sheen as "America's most distinguished pulpit orator" and "probably the best known of any Catholic priest in America, excluding cardinals and archbishops, whose record for convert making is unequalled in America, and who would add prestige to the office." (Actually, Monsignor Sheen was better known than the cardinals and archbishops, too.) The Vatican, however, did not appoint Monsignor Sheen to that post.

On that trip in 1948, both Cardinal Spellman and Monsignor Sheen kept diaries. They described huge crowds everywhere they stopped. Those stops included Hawaii, the Fiji Islands, Australia, New Zealand, Java, Singapore, the Philippines, China, and Japan. By the end of the trip, which lasted fifty-two days, they had traveled forty-three thousand miles. During that time, Monsignor Sheen delivered more than two hundred speeches, lectures, and sermons.

The cardinal and monsignor developed a mutual admiration for each other during this trip. Monsignor Sheen wrote in his diary that he was amazed at how well-known his name was in Australia. He also wrote about Cardinal Spellman, "There is absolutely no jealousy in that man."

Cardinal Spellman, for his part, expressed amusement at the attention Monsignor Sheen attracted. The cardinal, well aware that he was not the orator that the monsignor was, was quite willing to stand aside and let his protégé do the talking. Monsignor Sheen later confided to Clare Boothe Luce, "I know now why the Cardinal invited me. He tosses out the first ball and then asks me to pitch the rest of the game."

———

In 1950, Cardinal Spellman succeeded in getting the Vatican to appoint Monsignor Sheen national director of the Pontifical Mission Aid Societies in the United States, known as the Society for the Propagation of the Faith. The primary purpose of the Society is to raise money to support the Catholic Church's worldwide missionary activities. He resigned from his teaching role at Catholic University in Washington after twenty-four years, and moved to New York. "My entire energies," Monsignor Sheen said at the time, "will be dedicated to this work, which has the unique value of contributing to the peace of the world through peace of soul." When he wrote his autobiography, he said, "It was very consoling to have a universal mission and to consider the world as my parish."

He did indeed throw his energies into the work of the Society. For sixteen years he wrote and spoke about the importance of the Church's missions. During those sixteen years the Society raised nearly 200 million dollars. He increased donations from 3.5 million dollars when he became director in 1950 to nearly 16 million dollars in 1965. Americans were contributing almost two-thirds of the money collected in the world.

In 1951, Monsignor Sheen was appointed auxiliary bishop to Cardinal Spellman. Thus, when he began his famous television program about eight months later, he was known as Bishop Sheen.

Unfortunately, the good relationship between Cardinal Spellman and Bishop Sheen didn't last. There were two instances in which the two men disagreed over the use of money by the Society for the

Propagation of the Faith. The first happened in 1955, when the U.S. government made surplus food available to Catholic Relief Services to be distributed in countries recovering from World War II. Since the food was to be distributed by missionaries, Cardinal Spellman asked Bishop Sheen to provide funds from the Society to pay the expenses for distribution. Bishop Sheen refused, saying that he would do only what his superiors in Rome told him to do. The General Council of the Society rejected Cardinal Spellman's request.

The second instance also involved surplus food. For years the U.S. government had been giving Cardinal Spellman powdered milk, which he turned over to the Society for distribution to the world's poor. In 1957, the cardinal demanded that the Society pay millions of dollars for the supplies. Again Bishop Sheen refused. This time the dispute went all the way to Pope Pius XII, who listened to both prelates and sided with Bishop Sheen.

It is, of course, very unfortunate that two such great churchmen and patriots had to have a falling-out, but they did, and it affected the rest of Bishop Sheen's life. Cardinal Spellman turned against him. He tried, unsuccessfully, to get Pope Pius XII to replace Bishop Sheen as director of the Society for the Propagation of the Faith. He told Bishop Sheen that he would make him pastor of a wealthy parish in New York if he would resign as head of the Society, and the bishop refused.

Of course, the general public knew nothing about this. The cardinal and the bishop were always courteous toward each other. It was only insiders who knew about the antagonism. Bishop Sheen's annual Good Friday sermon at St. Patrick's Cathedral was canceled, and he delivered it in Jersey City. However, there were so many protests in New York that he was later returned to the schedule.

———

Perhaps no one admired Bishop Sheen's patriotism more than J. Edgar Hoover, the director of the Federal Bureau of Investigation. During his lifetime, Hoover was greatly admired for his anti-

Communism and for making the FBI a great investigative agency. It wasn't until after his death that the darker side of the man emerged.

The friendship between Sheen and Hoover began in 1944, during World War II, when Sheen continued to speak out against Communist Russia. When Monsignor Sheen said in one of his radio addresses that the Soviet Union was about to make a separate peace with Germany, an FBI agent was sent to find out where the monsignor got his information. Hoover followed up that visit with an invitation to dinner. By 1953 Bishop Sheen was on a private mailing list of people who received confidential information from the FBI, remaining on it at least through the 1960s.

Bishop Sheen spoke to groups of FBI agents several times, once at a Communion breakfast for more than a thousand personnel and another time to members of the FBI National Academy Association. He gave an inspirational patriotic speech in 1953 praising the FBI. He concluded it by saying:

> This great republic of ours chose not the serpent that crawls in the dust, not the lion that goes about seeking its prey that it might devour it, not the fox who overcomes its enemy by stealth. [America], in full consciousness of its own dignity and the full promise of what it was destined to be in the nations of the world, chose as its symbol the *Eagle*, flying onwards and upwards on to God.

Hoover sent numerous letters to the bishop congratulating him on some of his talks. He called the speech that is quoted above "one of the finest and most inspirational talks I have ever heard." For his part, Bishop Sheen called Hoover "one of the greatest men in our country today" and said that he was proud to be associated "with a department which is so truly American both in its tradition and in its outlook."

The bishop's biographer, Thomas Reeves, wrote in *America's Bishop*, "Just as Richard Nixon hornswoggled Billy Graham, presenting himself to the evangelist as a pious man of prayer, so J. Edgar Hoover, appearing to be the honest and selfless patriot, deceived Fulton J. Sheen."

The theme of patriotism popped up frequently in Bishop Sheen's books, sometimes in unexpected places. In 1949, for example, in his best-selling book *Peace of Soul,* he praised monks and nuns, saying that through their prayers they were "doing more for our country than all its politicians, its labor leaders, its army and navy put together; they are atoning for sins of us all." He wrote:

> The cloistered are the purest of patriots. They have not become less interested in the world since leaving it; indeed, they have become more interested in the world than ever before. But they are not concerned with whether it will buy and sell more; they care — and desperately care — whether it will be more virtuous and love God more.

It was front-page news when it was announced on October 26, 1966, that Bishop Sheen had been appointed bishop of Rochester, New York. Cardinal Spellman had succeeded in getting the man who was once his protégé, but later his adversary, out of New York City. At age seventy-one, he had to leave the Society for the Propagation of the Faith and head a relatively small diocese. Biographer Thomas Reeves called it his exile, and D. P. Noonan wrote a book about the years in Rochester that he called *The Passion of Fulton Sheen.*

Bishop Sheen had known about the appointment for six months, since he was asked to come to Rome and told about the decision to transfer him out of New York. He was given his choice of two archdioceses and five dioceses and chose Rochester. Before the appointment was announced, Bishop Sheen continued his whirlwind of activities. He traveled to Poland and Rome in May and preached retreats in Belfast, Northern Ireland, and Cork, Ireland, in July. He also taped a new television series (this time in color). It

181

was not the success that his programs were ten years earlier. He had lost some of his magic. (Videotapes of the programs are sold today under the title *Life Is Worth Living*. Purchasers often believe that they are buying the earlier programs.)

The years in Rochester were not happy ones. It was shortly after the end of the Second Vatican Council, in which Bishop Sheen had actively participated, and Rochester's new bishop tried to implement the teachings of that council. He, of course, had had no experience in administering a diocese, and this lack of experience was evident. He relied on other people as much as he could, but he was not accustomed to seeking advice, and his nature was such that he did what he wanted despite what others said.

He was not prepared, though, for a hostile local newspaper or criticism for the things he did. When he scheduled a series of retreat talks for the people of Rochester and rented the largest auditorium in the city, few people came. His disappointment was evident when he said privately, "The whole world comes to hear Fulton Sheen, except his own diocese." When he announced the closing of a school in Rochester, angry people appeared at a place he was going, pounding on his car and yelling obscenities. He reversed his decision the next day.

In 1967, Bishop Sheen decided to close an inner-city parish, St. Bridget's, and give the property to the U.S. government so it could erect housing for the poor. He made the offer to the Department of Housing and Urban Development, which accepted it early in 1968. When he announced the deal, he immediately ran into opposition from St. Bridget's parishioners as well as many of the diocese's priests. Pickets formed, and bitter phone calls and letters poured into the bishop's office. The Priests' Association of Rochester delivered a letter asking the bishop to rescind the offer.

Bishop Sheen wasn't prepared for anything like this. He was accustomed to being admired and popular. Now the people he was supposed to be leading were turning against him. He began to consider resigning as bishop because he believed his usefulness in Rochester was ended. He rescinded the offer to the government.

While he was in Rochester, he continued to make national head-lines from time to time. One of those times was in 1967 while America was in the middle of the Vietnam War. The war was not going well for American troops and anti-war demonstrations, especially on college campuses, were frequent. On July 30, from the pulpit of the cathedral in Rochester, Bishop Sheen called for the immediate with-drawal of American troops from Vietnam. It made the news because it was the first anti-Vietnam War statement by an American bishop. (It was also opposite the views which Cardinal Spellman expressed on numerous occasions.)

In May of 1969, Bishop Sheen met with Pope Paul VI and sub-mitted his resignation. The pope accepted the resignation later that year in October. At the same time, Pope Paul named him an arch-bishop, the titular bishop of the ancient see of Newport on the Isle of Wight. The bishop was then seventy-four, and the Vatican said he was retiring due to age. Archbishop Sheen, though, insisted that he was only resigning the diocese, not retiring. He said that he planned to return to New York "to teach any place I can, do TV, and enter into dialogue with unbelievers."

He had been Bishop of Rochester for three years. He later said in his autobiography that he regretted his failure to achieve more while he was there. He told Mike Wallace on a *60 Minutes* program that he had tried to carry out the teachings of Vatican II, and he said, "I was never given a chance to administer a diocese before. I am a man of ideas. I have been thinking these problems through for many years; this was the first opportunity that I had to implement them."

Archbishop Sheen returned to New York and resumed his active life. He wrote three more books (not counting his autobiography, which was published after his death), traveled extensively (thirty thousand miles in January and February of 1974) to give retreats and lectures, and delivered sermons to packed congregations. He even taped another television series when he was eighty years old, this one for a public broadcasting station in Toledo, Ohio. The thirteen programs were called *What Now America?*, and the first program was devoted to patriotism. The series was offered to PBS stations, but few of them picked it up. Television had changed too much since the 1950s. In 1976, when he was eighty-one, he spoke to six thousand people in the Las Vegas Convention Center for the celebration of America's bicentennial.

By the '70s, the Archbishop Sheen's health began to fade. He spent three weeks in Lenox Hospital in New York in 1974 after an attack of hiccups during a talk in Albany. In 1977, he underwent open-heart surgery, and a pacemaker was installed in his chest. Later that year he had to undergo prostate surgery. He had to spend four months in the hospital in 1978.

Still, he continued to work. In January of 1979, he spoke at the National Prayer Breakfast in Washington, D.C., at the invitation of President Jimmy Carter. Billy Graham was ready to fill in if Archbishop Sheen was unable to speak. Graham wrote later in his autobiography, "Even as he made his halting way to the podium, I silently prayed that God would grant him the necessary physical and spiritual strength. He then went on to preach one of the most challenging and eloquent sermons I have ever heard."

Archbishop Sheen began his talk in dramatic fashion. Turning toward President Carter, he said, "Mr. President, you are a sinner!" After a pause, he pointed to himself and said, "I am a sinner." After another pause, he indicated all the people in the ballroom and said, "We are all sinners, and we all need to turn to God."

Like Billy Graham, Jimmy Carter also was inspired to write about Archbishop Sheen's lecture at that National Prayer Breakfast. He wrote:

> It was a real pleasure and an unforgettable experience for me to meet him in person, and I especially appreciated his coming to the National Prayer Breakfast while I was president. With the possible exception of Billy Graham, Bishop Sheen

was the most well-known and admired person there — including presidents and other dignitaries.

Archbishop Sheen was present when Pope John Paul II visited St. Patrick's Cathedral on October 2, 1979. After the pope made his entrance, Archbishop Sheen was led to the sanctuary, where he knelt before the pope. The pope helped him to his feet and embraced him warmly, to tremendous applause. Pope John Paul told him that he had written and spoken well of the Lord Jesus and that he was a loyal son of the Church. That was exactly what Archbishop Sheen had tried to do and be throughout his life.

Because of his lifetime devotion to the Blessed Virgin, Archbishop Sheen had said that he hoped he would die on one of her feast days. He almost got his wish. He died at age eighty-four on the evening of December 9, 1979, the day after the feast of the Immaculate Conception. His body was found in his chapel, before the Blessed Sacrament.

Cardinal John J. O'Connor

My contribution [to my country] was a piece of my heart
… a piece of my heart.

— *CARDINAL JOHN J. O'CONNOR*

CHAPTER 9

Cardinal John J. O'Connor

By 1984, the Catholic Church in the United States was a mature Church, much more confident and willing to assert itself in the mainstream of the country's social life than it had been earlier in American history. Its leaders were now secure enough to make their opinions known not only to American Catholics, but also to society in general. The previous year, the U.S. bishops had issued a landmark pastoral letter called *The Challenge of Peace*, which was a forceful analysis of America's defense policy, especially on the issue of the use of nuclear weapons.

Archbishop John Joseph O'Connor, who had been a member of the bishops' committee that drafted the pastoral letter, had just been installed as archbishop of New York on March 19, 1984. And 1984 was an election year — an election year, according to *Time* magazine's September 10, 1984, issue in which "the prominence and complexity of religious issues may [be] greater than in any previous election."

Ronald Reagan and Walter Mondale were opposing each other for the presidency, and Reagan believed, as he said, that "faith and religion play a central role in the political life of our nation and always have." He stressed issues such as abortion, which he opposed, and prayer in public schools, which he supported. The Democratic Party's platform, on the other hand, supported the right of a woman to have an abortion.

In New York, Governor Mario Cuomo, a Catholic and the keynote speaker at the Democratic convention that year, presented a platform that supported legal abortion. The Democratic candidate for vice president, Geraldine Ferraro, also a Catholic, defended the right of a woman to have an abortion. Both claimed that they *personally* accepted the Church's teaching on abortion, but could not impose their beliefs on others.

In June of 1984, just three months after being installed, Archbishop O'Connor was quoted in *The New York Times* as saying that he could not see "how a Catholic in conscience could vote for an individual explicitly expressing himself or herself as favoring abortion."

Governor Cuomo quickly responded that Archbishop O'Connor had stepped over the line by telling Catholics how to vote. "Now you have the archbishop of New York," he said, "saying that no Catholic can vote for Ed Koch, no Catholic can vote for ... Pat Moynihan, or Mario Cuomo — anybody who disagrees with him on abortion."

Archbishop O'Connor replied:

> It is neither my responsibility nor my desire to evaluate the qualifications of any individual or any party for any public office, or of any individual holding public office. My sole responsibility is to present as clearly as I can the formal official teaching of the Catholic Church. I leave to those interested in such teachings whether or not the public statements of officeholders and candidates accord with this teaching.

Besides answering Governor Cuomo, Archbishop O'Connor also replied to an assertion by Geraldine Ferraro that "the Catholic position on abortion is not monolithic, and there can be a range of personal and political responses to it." The archbishop objected strenuously:

> Geraldine Ferraro has said some things relevant to Catholic teaching which are not true. ... The only thing I know about her is that she has given the world to understand that Catholic teaching is divided on the subject of abortion ...

As an officially approved teacher of the Catholic Church, all I can judge is that what has been said about Catholic teaching is wrong. It's wrong.

Ferraro continued to insist that many Catholics agreed with her position and criticized "people [who] try to use religion for their partisan political advantage." Cuomo, for his part, continued the controversy with a speech at the University of Notre Dame in which he tried to defend his point of view. Archbishop O'Connor responded to that speech (with Mother Teresa at his side) with a talk entitled "Human Lives, Human Rights." He called on politicians to commit themselves to changing the permissive abortion laws of the United States.

While this controversy was raging, Archbishop O'Connor issued a Labor Day statement in which he defended the Catholic Church's right to speak out on important issues of the day. He wrote:

As a "public Church," we believe that we have not only the right but the responsibility to contribute to the public debate on major issues of our day ... In doing so, the Church is not "intruding" in political affairs or adding an alien issue to the public debate. Rather it is seeking to make clear the human and moral consequences of the technical choices we make as a nation.

This controversy, at the very start of his years as archbishop, demonstrates that Archbishop O'Connor was a courageous defender of Catholic doctrine, especially when it came to the issue of abortion. In years to come, Cardinal O'Connor would be chairman of the U.S. Conference of Catholic Bishops' Committee for Pro-Life Activities from 1989 to 1992, during which he inaugurated a five million dollar public information campaign on abortion.

In his very first statement as archbishop of New York, O'Connor pledged to devote himself unceasingly to "efforts to defend human life, especially the life of the unborn. Such efforts will constitute my number-one priority and will permeate everything I attempt to do."

He followed up that statement on October 15, 1984, with another bold one — he said that any pregnant woman in crisis, regardless of background or religion, could contact him and receive free medical care, assistance in keeping her baby, adoption services, and legal help if needed.

In his zeal for the pro-life movement, Cardinal O'Connor used his column in *Catholic New York*, the archdiocesan newspaper, to propose the formation of a community of women consecrated to the support of human life in all its stages. His proposal drew an enthusiastic response from women, so in 1991 he founded the Sisters of Life. By the time of the cardinal's death in 2000, the new order had forty-five members, including four who were fully professed and twenty-four in first vows.

He wasn't afraid to take to the streets in support of pro-life causes. In 1992, he led a procession and prayer session in front of Manhattan's busiest abortion clinic. Each year, too, he went to Washington in January to participate in the March for Life held on the anniversary of the Supreme Court's Roe v. Wade decision that legalized abortion.

Cardinal O'Connor asked the Knights of Columbus to sponsor monuments to the unborn child in every diocese in the United States. By the time of his death, there were almost two thousand such memorials in the United States, Canada, and the Philippines.

Naturally, he was often criticized for his pro-life position. Once, at a Harvard Law School forum, he noted the charge that the Catholic Church was attempting to impose its teachings on others. He asked, "Why would we bishops not be imposing our morality on others when we oppose rape, but impose our morality on others when we oppose abortion?"

His anti-abortion stance was undoubtedly what Cardinal O'Connor was most well-known for. At Cardinal O'Connor's funeral, Cardinal Bernard Law gave the homily. When he made reference to

Cardinal O'Connor's defense of human life, thunderous applause broke out for almost two minutes.

———

This, though, is a book about patriotism. Cardinal O'Connor's patriotism was best exemplified by his twenty-seven years as a Navy chaplain. He enlisted in the Navy as a chaplain in 1952, during the Korean conflict, and rose through the ranks to become a rear admiral and the Navy Chief of Chaplains in 1975. He retired from the military in 1979 when Pope John Paul II appointed him auxiliary bishop of New York and vicar general of the Military Ordinariate (now known as the Archdiocese for the Military Services).

Father O'Connor served on naval vessels in the Atlantic, Caribbean, and Mediterranean, ashore in various posts, and overseas in Korea, Japan, and Vietnam.

Father O'Connor became known as "the conscience of the Navy." He received the Legion of Merit twice. The first time was in 1958 for developing the Navy Moral Leadership Program, a two-volume work that is still a basic reference in the military. The second time was in 1965 for "exceptional meritorious conduct" as a chaplain to the Third Marine Division during the Vietnam War. In 1968 he wrote a book, *A Chaplain Looks at Vietnam*, which showed his patriotism. He argued that the war in Vietnam was necessary because the alternative would be a Communist takeover.

Although the book shows his patriotism at the time, he later said that he regretted having written the book. In 1985, he told Nat Hentoff, according to a column Hentoff wrote for *The New Republic*, "I wasn't aware that so many of the decisions leading to the enormous cost in lives and resources on both sides were taken for political rather than military reasons."

Father O'Connor was immensely popular with his sailors and marines. According to Archbishop Edwin F. O'Brien, currently head of the Archdiocese for the Military Services, when Father O'Connor began his service on the USS Canberra in the early 1960s, only about forty people attended his first Mass. When he left the ship twenty-two months later, four hundred were present.

In 1972, Father O'Connor became the first Catholic chief chaplain at the U.S. Naval Academy in Annapolis, Maryland. While there, he developed an ethics course for midshipmen and a video-cassette series of religious instructions that was used by Catholic military chaplains around the world. In 1975 he became the Navy Chief of Chaplains and served in that capacity for four years.

Archbishop O'Brien, who had served as Cardinal O'Connor's secretary, once asked the cardinal what he thought he gave to the country and the military during his twenty-seven years of service. Cardinal O'Connor replied, "My contribution was a piece of my heart … a piece of my heart … I hoped that in each place I went I helped save some souls, I got some marriages validated, I brought some people back to the Church. I hoped that each place I went, I improved the image of the Church a little bit."

Archbishop O'Brien celebrated a special Mass attended by Navy chaplains the day before the cardinal's funeral. He said this about the cardinal and his service to his country:

> More than half of his priestly life was selflessly dedicated to our men and women in uniform, serving as a Navy and Marine chaplain, and later as auxiliary bishop and administrator of the Military Vicariate (also known as the Military Ordinariate, now the Archdiocese for the Military Services). Whether interacting with an admiral or general, seaman or grunt Marine, spouse or child, he was their devoted, brave champion, their faithful friend. I have known no other whom so many call "my friend." His profound influence upon not only Catholics, but also God's people of all faith groups is his living legacy.

John Joseph O'Connor was born on January 15, 1920, in Philadelphia. He attended Saint Charles Borromeo Seminary and was ordained for the Archdiocese of Philadelphia on December 15, 1945. He taught high school for seven years while earning master's degrees in advanced ethics at Villanova University and in clinical psychology at The Catholic University of America in Washington, D.C. Later, he earned a doctorate in political science at Georgetown University.

After his twenty-seven years in the Navy, while he was an auxiliary bishop of New York and vicar general of the Military Ordinariate, Bishop O'Connor delivered a major paper on war and peace in Catholic teaching at an international meeting of military vicars. A month later, during the U.S. bishops' annual meeting in November of 1980, Bishop Francis P. Murphy of Baltimore suggested that the bishops publish a pastoral letter on war and peace. Bishop O'Connor was appointed to the committee to draft the letter. It was to become the most public and most debated letter the bishops ever wrote.

Archbishop Joseph Bernardin of Cincinnati (later the cardinal-archbishop of Chicago) was chairman of the committee that prepared the letter. Bishop O'Connor undoubtedly was appointed because of his experience in the Navy, and it was widely believed that he would support the views of the Reagan administration. At the opposite end was Auxiliary Bishop Thomas Gumbleton of Detroit, a pacifist. The primary author of the letter was Father J. Bryan Hehir, later dean of the Divinity School at Harvard University and still later head of U.S. Catholic Charities.

The letter was prepared over a period of two-and-a-half years and went through several drafts. By the time the second draft was published, the political climate in the United States was such that liberals were pushing for a freeze on nuclear weapons. Bishop O'Connor, though, was determined to keep the letter from being an endorsement of a partisan position. In particular, he objected to wording that called for a halt to "the testing, production, and deployment of new strategic weapons." At his suggestion, the committee changed the word "halt" to "curb." According to James Castelli in his book *Bishops and the Bomb*, "O'Connor had found the one word that would change the interpretation of the entire document in a politically charged, media heavy climate."

The letter that the bishops approved in May of 1983, *The Challenge of Peace: God's Promise and Our Response*, strongly rejected the use of nuclear weapons. It said, "We do not perceive any situation in which the deliberate initiation of nuclear warfare, on a however restricted scale, can be morally justified. Non-nuclear attacks by another state must be resisted by other than nuclear means." This was a statement that Bishop O'Connor could approve.

Although Bishop O'Connor was sometimes portrayed as a "hawk" when it came to nuclear weapons, he thought differently. "I would like to see every nuclear weapon disappear from the face of the earth," he said. "But that's not going to happen. We have to be rational about it. I never sincerely felt myself to be hawkish." He did, however, consider himself realistic.

In June of 1984, Bishop O'Connor and Cardinal Bernardin testified jointly before Congress. They challenged the Reagan administration proposals for developing a space-based defense system and spending heavily on new nuclear weapons, and they opposed the deployment of cruise and Pershing missiles in Western Europe.

———·———

During the meeting at which the bishops approved their letter on war and peace, Bishop O'Connor was walking toward a microphone to make a point. Archbishop Pio Laghi, the apostolic delegate to the United States, stopped him and told him, "The Holy Father has just appointed you bishop of Scranton."

After his installation in Scranton on June 29, 1983, Bishop O'Connor energetically threw himself into his new responsibilities

— so much so that *The Scranton Times* named him newsmaker of the year. He established boards, councils, and task forces to promote education, help the homeless, and foster ecumenical dialogue. He established the diocese's first communications department and began to visit every parish in the diocese.

His time in Scranton, however, lasted only seven months. On January 16, 1984, Archbishop Laghi called Bishop O'Connor on the phone. After a pleasant chat, the archbishop said casually, "By the way, the Holy Father has appointed you archbishop of New York."

The appointment took everyone by surprise, especially since Bishop O'Connor had so recently been appointed bishop of Scranton. It has been reported that Pope John Paul II told intimates, "I want somebody like me in New York." Whether or not the pope actually said that, there's no doubt that the archbishop and the pope did think and act alike. The pope relied heavily on O'Connor. He admitted as much after the cardinal's death when he said that he received the news of the cardinal's death "with a deep sense of personal loss." He said, too, "Through the years he has been of great support to me in the service of the universal Church."

The pope named Archbishop O'Connor a cardinal and installed him in the College of Cardinals on May 25, 1985. He also appointed him to the Congregation of Bishops, the first of many memberships in top Vatican agencies. It was as a member of the Congregation of Bishops that he was able to exert great influence on the selection of bishops for American dioceses for the next fifteen years. He seldom missed the congregation's monthly meetings, flying across the Atlantic Ocean to attend them.

Through the years, Cardinal O'Connor was also named to the Pontifical Commission (later Council) for Social Communications, the Council for the Public Affairs of the Church, the Pontifical Commission for Pastoral Assistance to Health Care Workers, the Council of Cardinals and Bishops of the Secretariat of State, the Congregation for Eastern Rite Churches, the Congregation for the Evangelization of Peoples, the Pontifical Council for the Family, and the Pontifical Council for Migrants and Travelers. The pope also appointed him co-president of the 1994 World Synod of Bishops on the Consecrated Life.

When a bishop or archbishop reaches the age of seventy-five, he must submit his resignation. Cardinal O'Connor did so when he reached that age and waited for Pope John Paul II to accept it. The pope, however, did not accept it. On St. Patrick's Day of 1995, when the cardinal returned to his office after leading New York's parade, he found a letter from the pope in which the pope refused to accept the resignation. Cardinal O'Connor served another five years.

———

It didn't take long after his installation as archbishop of New York for Cardinal O'Connor to begin making the impression on New York that Pope John Paul II expected. The media loved him because he was accessible, plain-spoken, and had a sense of humor. During his first press conference after being appointed archbishop, he was called to the phone. Rome was calling. When he returned to the press conference, he said solemnly, "I regret to inform you that the Holy Father has changed his mind." His charming of the New York press corps had started.

For years Cardinal O'Connor said Mass and gave a homily almost every Sunday at St. Patrick's Cathedral. He met with the press after Mass, and usually made news. He also wrote a weekly column in *Catholic New York* called "From My Viewpoint." His column ranged from personal anecdotes about his childhood, to a sharp denunciation of partial-birth abortion, to a lengthy series of columns on the Sacrament of Matrimony.

In 1988, he began a weekly, half-hour television series titled "Face to Face with John Cardinal O'Connor." It ran for eighteen months. He saw all of this as his most important responsibility — to impart the teachings of the Church to the widest audience possible.

Cardinal O'Connor was not afraid to take a stand against immorality no matter whose toes he stepped on. One of his first controversies was with the homosexual community. He made it clear that the Archdiocese of New York would not compromise on its teaching on the immorality of homosexual acts, even if it meant that its service agencies would have to give up millions of dollars in contracts with New York City.

New York Mayor Edward Koch had issued an order requiring agencies seeking city contracts to pledge not to discriminate in employment on the basis of "affectional preference." Archbishop O'Connor, however, refused to sign the pledge. He explained that although having a homosexual orientation is not in itself a sin, acting on such an orientation by committing homosexual acts is sinful. Therefore, the Church has a moral obligation to condemn homosexual activity by not employing openly active homosexuals.

Homosexual groups never forgave Cardinal O'Connor for his opposition to their behavior. In 1989, protesters interrupted his Sunday Mass and shouted him down so he couldn't finish his homily. They blocked the cathedral aisles, and at least one man threw a consecrated host on the floor and stepped on it. Cardinal O'Connor stopped his homily and led the congregation in the Rosary while police were restoring order. The police arrested forty-three demonstrators in the cathedral and sixty-eight others who tried to block the streets outside.

Cardinal O'Connor did try to reach out to homosexuals. Beginning in 1995, he held a dialogue twice a year in his office with members of Dignity, an organization of homosexual Catholics who disagree with Church teachings on sexual matters.

Meanwhile, the cardinal and Mayor Koch continued to disagree. The cardinal opposed the distribution of condoms in the public schools as an anti-AIDS measure. Despite their disagreements, though, the two men cooperated by co-authoring the book *His Emi-*

nence and Hizzoner in 1989. Each gave his views on controversial issues. Concerning his controversies with homosexual groups, for example, Cardinal O'Connor wrote:

> I recognize human weakness (in whom more than in myself?). I know that both heterosexual and homosexual can slip and fall every day, a dozen times a day or more. The Church asks only that with God's grace we pick ourselves up and start over again. The confessional exists not because we Catholics don't sin, but because we do.

Although he opposed the distribution of condoms as a way of combating AIDS, Cardinal O'Connor started several programs for people with AIDS. These included the first hospital-based dental clinic for AIDS patients, a residence for babies with AIDS, and an acute care unit at St. Clare's Hospital in Manhattan for prisoners with AIDS. In 1987 President Reagan appointed him to a national commission on AIDS.

The cardinal didn't just start programs; he also went to the people. In order to learn more about the dreaded AIDS disease, he spent many hours at St. Clare's Hospital as a hands-on volunteer. He even accepted the task of emptying bedpans. Cardinal O'Connor was also well-known at Manhattan's Memorial Sloan-Kettering Cancer Center and other New York hospitals for his frequent visit to patients.

———

Cardinal O'Connor shared with Pope John Paul II a concern for both the Jews and Palestinians. As president of the Catholic Near East Welfare Association since 1984, he traveled to the Middle East several times for meetings with both political and religious leaders. In 1989, he and two other archbishops drafted a major statement for the U.S. bishops' conference that advocated a Palestinian homeland as essential for achieving a lasting peace in the area.

The cardinal unintentionally created a diplomatic stir in 1987 when he scheduled meetings with Israeli officials in their offices in Jerusalem. At the time, the Vatican did not have diplomatic relations with Israel and did not recognize Jerusalem as the capital of Israel. Cardinal O'Connor quickly switched the meetings to the officials' homes instead of their offices.

However, during another trip to the Middle East at the end of 1991 and the start of 1992, after meetings with King Hussein of Jordan and the presidents of Egypt and Lebanon, the cardinal went ahead with a meeting with Israeli President Yitzhak Shamir in his office in Jerusalem. He told reporters who questioned him that changes in relations between Israel and the Vatican were going to come, at the insistence of the pope. The Vatican and Israel formally signed an agreement that led to full diplomatic relations in 1993. This allowed Pope John Paul II to visit Israel, during which time he apologized to the Jews for the anti-Semitism that existed in the Catholic Church during various periods of history. The pope visited the Yad Vashem Holocaust Memorial and prayed at the Western Wall of the Temple Mount in Jerusalem.

Cardinal O'Connor followed the example of the pope when he wrote a letter to some Jewish friends in which he said he hoped for "a new era" in Catholic-Jewish relations. On behalf of Catholics, he expressed his sorrow for "the pain inflicted on the Jewish people by many of our members over the last millennium." With the cardinal's permission, the letter was published as a full-page advertisement in *The New York Times*.

In explaining to Catholics how they should feel toward the Jews, Cardinal O'Connor wrote in his book *On Being Catholic*, "To say to Jews, 'Forget the Holocaust,' is to say to Christians, 'Forget the crucifixion.' There is a 'sacramentality' about the Holocaust for Jews all over the world. It constitutes a mystery by definition beyond their understanding — or ours."

The cardinal was episcopal moderator of the U.S. bishops' committee on Catholic-Jewish relations from 1992 to 1995, and Jewish groups recognized his efforts on behalf of improved Catholic-Jewish relations. The Anti-Defamation League presented him with the Cardinal Bea Interfaith Award and the American Jewish Committee gave him the Isaiah Interreligious Award. The American Jewish Committee praised the cardinal for "his remarkable leadership in building human bridges of solidarity between Catholics and Jews."

It continued:

> The cardinal was at the forefront in the struggle to free Soviet Jews, to eradicate every vestige of anti-Semitism, to commemorate the Holocaust, and to establish diplomatic relations between the Vatican and the state of Israel ... During his distinguished tenure as New York's archbishop, the cardinal worked closely with us on a host of issues, including healing the wounds of war in the Balkans and strengthening human rights throughout the world.

After Cardinal O'Connor's death, Dr. Ronald B. Sobel, senior rabbi for Congregation Emanu-El of New York City, said of him, "No one in the American Catholic hierarchy, past or present, has been as caring and faithful a friend to the Jewish people as was His Eminence."

———

In addition to his diplomatic adventures in the Middle East, Cardinal O'Connor was also involved in trying to improve relations with Cuba. In 1988 he had a marathon late-night meeting with Cuba's President Fidel Castro that laid the initial groundwork for the visit to Cuba by Pope John Paul II ten years later.

During the meeting in 1988, Cardinal O'Connor expressed concerns about Cuba's political prisoners. About two months later, Castro sent the cardinal a list of four hundred thirty-three political prisoners he was willing to release. Some of them were men whose freedom the Catholic Church had sought for many years.

Cardinal O'Connor accompanied the pope on his trip to Cuba. Besides attending the Masses, ceremonies, and receptions that are a regular part of papal trips, the cardinal also found the opportunity to offer Mass for seven contemplative Carmelite nuns in their convent in Havana. He had been helping these nuns since the early 1980s when they wrote to him asking for help for one of their sisters who could not walk because of knee problems. Cardinal O'Connor arranged for the sister to go to New York for surgery. Later, he arranged for other things that the cloistered nuns needed, including eyeglasses, religious articles, and a machine to make Communion wafers.

—·—

Another area in which Cardinal O'Connor took an active interest was that of labor relations. As the son of a painter who was a member of a union, he was an outspoken advocate for the right of workers to unionize. In 1989, during contract negotiations with Catholic school teachers in the Archdiocese of New York, he defended the right of the teachers to organize. During the annual archdiocesan Labor Mass in St. Patrick's Cathedral, he told archdiocesan workers who felt that they were being treated unjustly that they were free to picket him at his residence or office. However, he drew the line at pickets while he was celebrating Mass, saying that would show disrespect to Christ.

In 1990, when unionized workers at the *New York Daily News* went on strike, he publicly supported the strikers. He also submitted testimony to the U.S. Congress supporting legislation that would prevent employers from hiring permanent workers to replace strikers. He said that hiring permanent replacements "can make a charade of collective bargaining and a mockery of the right to strike."

In 1994 and 1995, the issue of hiring permanent replacements for workers struck close to home. During a long strike by nurses at a Mercy Sisters' hospital in the Archdiocese of New York, the management of the hospital thought about hiring replacements. Cardinal O'Connor made it clear that doing so would be in opposition to archdiocesan policy. Nat Hentoff reported that he was in a corridor outside the cardinal's office when "I heard O'Connor roaring, 'Over my dead body will any person be fired because he or she belongs to a union and is exercising the right of collective bargaining.'"

The cardinal was sometimes criticized by some of his best friends in the pro-life movement for his support of workers' rights. But Cardinal O'Connor didn't back off. The motto he chose when he became a bishop was "There can be no love without justice," and in one of his homilies he said pointedly, "There's no point in simply talking to people about filling their souls of you don't fill their bellies."

Nat Hentoff, who wrote a book about Cardinal O'Connor, was present at a dinner at which conservative business managers criticized the Church for its involvement in economic affairs. "What business is it of the Church," one man asked, "to get involved with the minimum wage, maximum employment, and such secular matters?"

Cardinal O'Connor answered:

> I am a priest. About nine hundred thousand individuals in New York City live in substandard conditions, including overcrowding, with all the attendant evils of that kind of life. I would be failing, as a priest, if all I did was to say Mass and carry out the customary religious duties of my office.

He was sometimes accused of speaking out too much on the subject of abortion while not saying enough about other issues. In the book he wrote with Mayor Koch, *His Eminence and Hizzoner*, he said:

> When I have pleaded on behalf of the life of the unborn, I have been accused of being indifferent to the problems of the poor, the homeless, the abused child or mother, or the dangers of nuclear war, or whatever, because in a particular address I have focused on the life of the unborn. Yet I have never once talked to any audience about any of these other

issues and been accused of being indifferent to the *unborn* for not mentioning them.

———•———

Cardinal O'Connor had enjoyed good health all his life. In 1999, however, he was diagnosed with a brain tumor that required surgery. The surgery was followed by radiation treatments that altered his appearance, making his face bloated and his head bald. Nevertheless, he returned to conduct the business of the archdiocese as soon as he could, first from his residence and then back in his office. He celebrated Midnight Mass on Christmas and gave a full homily even though his radiation treatments slurred his speech.

He even made one more trip to the Vatican in February of 2000, during which he had a final meeting with Pope John Paul II. After that, his health began to decline seriously.

In March, the U.S. Congress voted to award Cardinal O'Connor the Congressional Gold Medal, the nation's highest civilian honor. Senator Charles Schumer and Representative Vito Fossella of New York presented the medal to the cardinal on March 6, 2000. The proclamation lauded the cardinal for his outstanding services to the United States — a fitting tribute to the patriotic prelate.

Cardinal O'Connor died peacefully at his residence on May 3, 2000, at the age of eighty. Tributes came pouring in from throughout the world. President Bill Clinton, with whom the cardinal had disagreed on many issues, wrote:

> For more than fifty years, he reached out with uncommon fortitude to minister to the needs of American Catholics. From his first Philadelphia parish to soldiers on the battlefield, from the carnage of Bosnia to the tragedy of AIDS, he also sought out and served those most in need. His lifelong journey of faith was our nation's blessing. From his distinguished career as a Navy chaplain, to his determination to give voice to the poor and marginalized in New York and across Amer-

ica, the courage and firm faith he showed in his final illness inspired us all.

Both President Clinton and former president George Herbert Walker Bush were among the dignitaries who attended the funeral.

It was another cardinal of the Church, though, who recognized Cardinal O'Connor's patriotism. Cardinal James A. Hickey of Washington, after learning about Cardinal O'Connor's death, noted his love for the Holy Father, his loyalty to the Church, his readiness to serve people in every condition of life, and his role as a leading spokesman for the Church on vitally important issues. He further commented, "His Eminence will also be remembered as a patriot who deeply loved his country and devoted much of his pastoral ministry to the men and women of the armed services, eventually rising to the rank of rear admiral and becoming Navy Chief of Chaplains."

Cardinal O'Connor's life showed once again that the greatest priests and prelates of the Catholic Church in the United States were also its greatest patriots.

Archbishop John Purcell

I have taken an oath to support the Constitution of the United States. I cannot take another.

— *FATHER GABRIEL RICHARD*

CHAPTER 10

Additional Catholic Patriots

This book does not attempt to list all of the United States Catholic churchmen who have demonstrated their patriotism. Rather, by giving the stories of a few of the more famous American Catholic churchmen, it illustrates that patriotism is a quality that can be found in any good Catholic — whether he be a clergyman or a layman. Indeed, since the virtue of patriotism is really an internal virtue, the most lowly priest in the smallest of parishes, or one of his least known parishioners, could very well have more patriotism than those written about here. There have been many, many Catholics in the history of the United States who have demonstrated great patriotism.

During the Revolutionary War, for example, the activities of **Father Peter Gibault** were of major importance to America, for it was through his influence that Colonel George Rogers Clark was able to take possession of the Illinois country and thus secure it for the United States in the final peace treaty.

The main settlements in the Illinois country were Kaskaskia, at the mouth of the Kaskaskia River on the Mississippi, about fifty miles south of St. Louis; Prairie de Rocher, about seventeen miles north of Kaskaskia; Cahokia, north again and just below modern East St. Louis; and Vincennes on the Wabash in present-day Indiana. After Colonel Clark had managed to capture Kaskaskia, Prairie du

Rocher, and Cahokia, the inhabitants of those settlements, mostly French Catholics, cast off allegiance to England when they received from Clark a firm guarantee of freedom of religion. Father Peter Gibault then volunteered to make the long journey to Vincennes to try to talk his fellow Frenchmen there into also allying themselves with the United States. He was completely successful, and in August of 1778 Clark sent a small force to occupy Vincennes.

Later, the British managed to recapture Vincennes, and the morale of the people of Kaskaskia and Cahokia was lower than ever. But Father Gibault helped Colonel Clark argue and plead with the people to such an extent that some of the local population joined Clark's men in marching to Vincennes through a bitter winter to capture the town a second time. This was accomplished on February 24, 1779, and the Illinois country remained in U.S. hands throughout the rest of the war.

Father Gibault's actions brought him a formal citation from the legislature of Virginia. They also, however, brought him the censure of his bishop, Jean Briand, for this territory was under the ecclesiastical jurisdiction of Quebec, Canada.

———

There's a park in Detroit named after **Father Gabriel Richard**, complete with a large statue. The inscription under it summarizes Father Richard's contributions to Michigan. It reads:

> Father Gabriel Richard, 1767–1832. Pioneer priest-patriot. Founder of churches and schools, co-founder of the University of Michigan, member of Congress, printer, martyr of charity, prophet and apostle of Christian civilization. He served God and country on the Michigan frontier.

During the War of 1812, the British occupied Detroit and demanded that all citizens take an oath of allegiance to the British crown. Father Richard denounced the British from his pulpit and said, "I have taken an oath to support the Constitution of the United States. I cannot take another." The British arrested him, deported him to Windsor, Ontario, and kept him under house arrest until the end of the war.

Father Richard was a Sulpician priest who escaped from France at the time of the French Revolution. After working in Illinois, he joined many other French people in Detroit in 1798. Journalist Malcolm Bingay called him "the soul of the city."

He founded the University of Michigan and persuaded his friend, Dr. John Montieth, a Presbyterian minister, to become its first president. At the beginning, the two men divided the 13 classes offered between them. Before Montieth arrived in Detroit in 1816, Father Richard had gathered Detroit's Protestants together on Sunday afternoons and preached to them. He was an early exponent of ecumenism.

Father Richard founded Michigan's first newspaper, *The Michigan Essay and Impartial Observer*. To publish it, he imported the first printing press to come west of the Alleghenies. He also used the press to print schoolbooks and catechisms. He founded elementary schools, a school to train farmers, and a school to train teachers. He also organized Detroit's first circulating library.

In 1823, Father Richard became the first priest to become a member of the U.S. Congress after Michigan was organized as a territory. While in Congress he succeeded in getting the federal government to build a road from Detroit to Chicago.

———

During the Civil War, Archbishop John Hughes was not the only Catholic prelate who upheld the cause of the Union. After Hughes died during that war, much of the Catholic leadership in the North passed to **Archbishop John Purcell** of Cincinnati. Of course, he had not been completely quiet before Hughes' death, for as early as 1861 the *Freeman's Journal* reported him as saying, "The Catholic Church is conservative, and all its principles revolve and gravitate around the idea of union. What is the principle of secession but the carrying out of the principle of private judgment?"

Through his diocesan newspaper, the *Telegraph*, Archbishop Purcell urged loyalty to the Union and supported President Lincoln's Emancipation Proclamation, stating, "If the question of American slavery were to be submitted tomorrow to a general council of the Church, the institution would perish — sunken deeper than ever plummet sounded."

———·———

As we have seen, Archbishop Ireland received the Medal of Honor for his heroism as a chaplain during the Civil War. Other chaplains for the North during the Civil War also distinguished themselves in many ways.

One of the most noted of the chaplains was **Father William Corby** of the University of Notre Dame. He joined General Thomas Meagher's New York Irish Brigade, almost all of whom were Catholics. He served in that regiment in the battles of Fair Oaks, Antietem, Fredericksburg, Chancellorsville, and Gettysburg. At Antietem, he rode up and down the lines admonishing the soldiers to be sorry for their sins before he imparted general absolution. Before the Battle of Gettysburg, he climbed on a large rock, gave a patriotic speech reminding the soldiers of their duty to God and country, and gave general absolution. A bronze statue of Father Corby was erected at Gettysburg in 1910. A duplicate of the statue is in front of Corby Hall at Notre Dame.

The Irish Brigade, by the way, began with 3,000 men. By 1863, it was reduced to only 530 active troops, the others having been killed or wounded. At the Battle of Gettysburg, 198 men of the Irish Brigade were killed.

A colleague of Father Corby at Notre Dame, **Father Paul Gillen**, began his career as a chaplain in an unofficial capacity. He bought a buggy in which he piled his supplies, and he followed the army wherever he felt his services might be needed. He slept in the buggy and used it as his chapel. One day, General Grant came across this nonmilitary and unauthorized vehicle within the lines and promptly had Father Gillen arrested. Gillen later accepted a regular commission and served the remainder of the war in an official capacity.

Father Thomas Ouellet, a Jesuit, distinguished himself during the Battle of Malvern Hill by going along the battlefront with a lantern asking each wounded man he encountered, "Are you a Catholic? Do you wish absolution?"

Following the Civil War, there was considerable bitterness still existing between the people of the North and those of the South. Nevertheless, this was precisely the time when **Archbishop Martin John Spalding** of Baltimore called, and presided at, the Second Plenary Council of Baltimore. When this council convened in the autumn of 1866, the country was amazed that the bishops of the North and South could actually get together for a peaceful discussion of their problems. This was, as a matter of fact, one of the reasons Archbishop Spalding called the council. He considered it opportune,

> that at the close of the national crisis, which had acted as a dissolvent upon all sectarian ecclesiastical organizations, the Catholic Church might present to the country and the world a striking proof of the strong bond of unity with which her members are knit together.

He felt, too, that this council, showing that the bishops of the North and South could work together, would aid in getting the other citizens of the country together again.

This council, among many other things (the proceedings and decrees enunciated take up almost four hundred pages), counseled the citizens of the United States to maintain the duty of obedience to civil authority. The bishops stated:

For the children of the Church, obedience to the civil power is not a submission to force which may not be resisted; nor merely the compliance with a condition for peace and security; but a religious duty founded on obedience to God, by whose authority the civil magistrate exercises his power.

Archbishop Spalding also used his influence to obtain from President Andrew Johnson a pardon for **Bishop Patrick Lynch** of Charleston, who had supported the Confederate States and had visited European countries to try to obtain support for the South.

———

During the "Era of Gibbons," there were four prelates who were known for their outstanding patriotism. Two of these, Cardinal James Gibbons and Archbishop John Ireland, have already been discussed at length. The other two were **Bishop John J. Keane** (later made an archbishop) and **Monsignor Denis J. O'Connell** (later made a bishop). These four men worked together through all the trials of that tumultuous time: the battle over the Knights of Labor, Cahenslyism, Americanism, etc.

Bishop Keane succeeded Cardinal Gibbons as bishop of Richmond and later became the first rector of The Catholic University of America. He and Archbishop Ireland helped Cardinal Gibbons write the cardinal's memorial to the Holy See about the Knights of Labor, and before that time he had spent considerable energy in Rome "laying the groundwork" for Cardinal Gibbons' visit.

Bishop Keane was also in Rome during the fight over the heresy of Americanism, of which he gave this definition:

Americanism is merely the sentiment of Catholics toward their country — a feeling of satisfaction, of gratitude, and of devotion to which Archbishop Carroll first gave expression. It is not a system nor a doctrinal program, nor any kind of propaganda.

It was Bishop Keane, too, who, after being asked to do it by the Holy See, cabled Archbishop Ireland requesting him to go to Washington to try to prevent the Spanish-American War.

When Keane, because of his outspokenness, was asked to resign as rector of Catholic University, there was considerable public resentment because he was widely known for his patriotism, his idealism, his success in winning converts to the Church, and for faithfully and diligently working for the success of Catholic University. Cardinal Gibbons took notice of this public esteem and the protests when he stated that the public resentment "proves the interest which the country takes in the affairs of the Catholic Church and also the great place that Monsignor Keane occupies in the esteem and affection of his fellow citizens."

Monsignor Denis J. O'Connell, rector of the American College in Rome, was so aggressively American that once during a Roman reception he refused to stand during the playing of "God Save the Queen." When Cardinal Gibbons took over his parish church in Rome after being made a cardinal, it was O'Connell who influenced him to speak about the benefits of America's separation of Church and State.

O'Connell was also instrumental in the fight against Cahenslyism. He and Archbishop Ireland stirred up public opinion against Cahensly — O'Connell in Rome and Ireland in the United States.

In the dispute over Americanism, Monsignor O'Connell was invited to explain the meaning of the term at the Fourth International Catholic Scientific Congress in Fribourg, Switzerland. After this speech, Gibbons told him that he was delighted with the explanation, and that

> every sentence conveys a pregnant idea, and the relations of Church and State are admirably set forth, especially for the eye of Rome. "If this be treason, let them make the most of it," to use the words of Patrick Henry. I must congratulate you on your success. I have often written and spoken on the subject, but you have gone more profoundly to the root.

In 1857, Father Isaac Hecker, in one of the two articles he wrote in Rome for *Civilta Cattolica*, predicted that some day the Catholic Church would look for missionaries from the United States to convert the Japanese and the Chinese. This prediction was to come true in 1911, when **Father James A. Walsh** and **Father Thomas F. Price** founded the Catholic Foreign Mission Society of America, widely known as Maryknoll. This was the first religious society founded in the United States to train missionaries to serve in other countries. To be sure, there had been U.S. citizens who became missionaries, but they had to join European societies in order to do so.

In naming their new organization, the two founders were careful to include "of America" in the title because they wanted to distinguish it from European groups and because it had received the sanction of the American hierarchy.

The sending of missionaries to other countries was certainly the mark of a mature Church in the United States. When the first priests were actually sent to China in 1918, under the leadership of Father Price, the highest councils of the Church were watching and waiting to see if these Americans would be able to survive the trials awaiting them in Asia. They were bringing with them the Americans' love for freedom of religion and an American system for bringing about results.

One of the group of four priests who were the first Maryknoll missionaries to China was a young man named **Father James Edward Walsh** (no relation to the co-founder of Maryknoll). He was later consecrated a bishop and became a symbol of the freedom of religion enjoyed in the free world.

In 1958 Bishop Walsh, called by his thousands of Chinese converts "the pillar of truth in China," was accused by the Chinese Communists of being an imperialist spy and was condemned at a trial he was not even permitted to attend. He was sentenced to twenty years in a Communist prison.

For eleven years prior to his trial, Bishop Walsh lived through what the American hierarchy called the worst persecution of Christians in all of its two thousand years. Nevertheless, Bishop Walsh chose to remain in China rather than abandon the people among whom he had labored. The Communists at first tried to get Bishop Walsh to leave China voluntarily. Finally, though, since his very presence kept religion alive among the Chinese people, they imprisoned him.

Protests to the imprisonment arose throughout the United States. The vice president of the United States, Richard Nixon, called the "trumped-up charges" a "Communist violation of human rights and freedom." Secretary of State Christian Herter said, "I find it difficult to emphasize sufficiently the revulsion I personally and the United States government feel." The *Baltimore Sun* said that the Chinese, knowing that Bishop Walsh could have avoided his suffering, would know why he stayed, and added, "So will free men everywhere in the world and those who would be free."

Bishop Walsh was eventually freed from prison and returned to the United States.

———•———

We have seen the contributions made by chaplains in the Civil War. This has been true of every war in which the United States has fought. In World War I, the most celebrated chaplain was **Father Francis P. Duffy**, who served the equally celebrated "Fighting Sixty-Ninth," the Irish regiment from New York City that became the 165th Infantry.

During World War I, Father Duffy worked closely with the commander of the "Fighting Sixty-Ninth," Colonel William Donovan. The legendary Colonel Donovan, known affectionately as "Wild Bill," was awarded the four highest decorations of the Army during World War I, and later headed the Office of Strategic Services during World War II.

After his services in World War I, Father Duffy wrote his autobiography, *Father Duffy's Story*. A movie was made of his exploits.

He went on to organize and build the Church of Our Savior in the Bronx and was pastor of the Church of the Holy Cross in New York until his death in 1932. A heroic bronze statue at the north end of Times Square in New York City depicts him as a chaplain.

This book would not be complete without a few more details about **Cardinal Francis J. Spellman**, archbishop of New York from 1939 to 1967. In the chapter about Archbishop Fulton J. Sheen, it was noted that Cardinal Spellman could easily rival Bishop Sheen when it came to patriotism. He was a personal friend of President Franklin Roosevelt, whom he greatly admired, but he had a personal quarrel with Eleanor Roosevelt, whom he once accused of having a "record of anti-Catholicism."

During World War II, Archbishop Spellman (he was named a cardinal in 1946) was also the nation's military vicar. As such, he oversaw 3,270 commissioned Catholic chaplains plus 2,018 civilian priests who served as auxiliary chaplains. But his greatest contributions to the soldiers were his personal travels to meet with them, say Mass for them, and listen to them. In 1941, he traveled eighteen thousand miles. Two years later, he covered forty-six thousand miles in twenty-four weeks, and in 1944 his European tour lasted three months. He visited troops in hospitals and near the battlefields, taking down the names of the soldiers so he could write letters to their families. One biographer estimated that the archbishop wrote "tens of thousands" of such letters.

Cardinal Spellman was also a staunch and outspoken opponent of Communism, frequently speaking out from the pulpit of St. Patrick's Cathedral. In October of 1946, for example, he warned that Communists in the United States were "tirelessly trying to grind into dust the blessed freedoms for which our sons have fought, sacrificed, and died."

On May 1, 1949, the Archdiocese of New York sponsored an anti-Soviet rally at New York's Polo Grounds. The featured speakers were Cardinal Spellman, Bishop Sheen, and Vice President Alben W. Barkley. The purpose of the meeting was to pledge the loyalty of all Catholics to the principles of the United States, to pray for those who were persecuting Christians behind the Iron Curtain, and to identify with the Christian victims of Communist persecution.

CHAPTER NOTES

Introduction — Patriotism and Catholicism

Besides my own judgments expressed in the Introduction, most of the material was derived from two books. The short history of the Catholic Church in the United States up to the year 1763 came from Theodore Roemer's *The Catholic Church in the United States* (B. Herder Book Co., St. Louis, 1950). Quotations in the third part of the Introduction were all found in Archbishop John F. Noll's *Decline of Nations* (Our Sunday Visitor Press, Huntington, Indiana, 1940).

Chapter 1 — Archbishop John Carroll

The following books were the primary sources for the chapter about Archbishop Carroll: John Gilmary Shea's *Life and Times of the Most Rev. John Carroll* (The Mershon Co. Press, Rahway, New Jersey, 1888), Joseph Gurn's *Charles Carroll of Carrollton* (P.J. Kenedy & Sons, New York, 1932), and Theodore Roemer's *The Catholic Church in the United States* (B. Herder Book Co., St. Louis, 1950).

Chapter 2 — Bishop John England

The following books were the primary sources for the chapter about Bishop England: Joseph L. O'Brien's *John England, Bishop of Charleston, The Apostle to Democracy* (The Edward O'Toole Co., New York, 1934), and Dorothy Fremont Grant's *John England: American Christopher* (Bruce Publishing Co., Milwaukee, 1949).

Chapter 3 — Archbishop John Hughes

The primary source for this chapter was Doran Hurley's *John Hughes, Eagle of the Church* (P.J. Kenedy & Sons, New York, 1961), with background supplied by Benjamin Blied's *Catholics and the Civil War* (Bruce Publishing Co., Milwaukee, 1945), John Gilmary Shea's *History of the Catholic Church in the United States, 1844 to 1866* (The Mershon Co. Press, Rahway, New Jersey, 1892), and Theodore Roemer's *The Catholic Church in the United States* (B. Herder Book Co., St. Louis, 1950).

Chapter 4 — Cardinal James Gibbons

The primary source for this chapter was John Tracy Ellis' *The Life of James Cardinal Gibbons* (Bruce Publishing Co., Milwaukee, 1952). Other sources, however, were also consulted frequently, including Arline Boucher and John Tehan's *Prince of Democracy* (Hanover House, Doubleday & Co., Garden City, New York, 1962), and Glenn D. Kittler's chapter on Cardinal Gibbons in his book *Profiles in Faith* (Coward-McGann, New York, 1962).

Chapter 5 — Archbishop John Ireland

The primary source for this chapter was James H. Moynihan's *The Life of Archbishop John Ireland* (Harper & Brothers, New York, 1952). In addition, John Tracy Ellis' *The Life of James Cardinal Gibbons* (Bruce Publishing Co., Milwaukee, 1952) also proved valuable for information about Archbishop Ireland.

Chapter 6 — Father Isaac Hecker

The sources that proved most valuable for this chapter were Vincent F. Holden's *The Yankee Paul* (Bruce Publishing Co., Milwaukee, 1958), Katherine Burton's *Celestial Homespun* (Longmans, Green and Co., New York, 1943), John A. O'Brien's *Giants of the Faith* (Hanover House, Doubleday & Co., Garden City, New York, 1957), John Tracy Ellis' *The Life of James Cardinal Gibbons* (Bruce Publishing Co., Milwaukee, 1952), and James H. Moynihan's *The Life of Archbishop John Ireland* (Harper & Brothers, New York, 1952).

Chapter 7 — Archbishop John F. Noll

The most valuable sources for this chapter included Richard Ginder's *With Ink and Crosier* (Our Sunday Visitor Press, Huntington, Indiana, 1952); the archbishop's many writings, particularly his books *The Decline of Nations, Civilization's Builder and Protector*, and *It Is Happening Here* (all published by Our Sunday Visitor Press); and copies of *Our Sunday Visitor*, May 5, 1912, through August 26, 1956, particularly the issue for August 12, 1956.

Chapter 8 — Archbishop Fulton J. Sheen

The primary sources for material in this chapter came from Thomas C. Reeves' biography of Archbishop Sheen, *America's Bishop: The Life and Times of Fulton J. Sheen* (Encounter Books, San Francisco, 2001), and *Treasure in Clay: The Autobiography of Fulton J. Sheen* (Doubleday, New York, 1980), as well as some of Archbishop Sheen's other books.

Chapter 9 — Cardinal John J. O'Connor

The primary sources for this chapter were the May 11, 2000, issue of *Catholic New York*, articles by Catholic News Service and in *The New York Times*, and Nat Hentoff's book *John Cardinal O'Connor: At the Storm Center of a Changing American Catholic Church* (Scribner, New York, 1988). Also useful were James Castelli's book *The Bishops and the Bomb: Waging Peace in a Nuclear Age* (Doubleday, New York, 1983), and Timothy A. Byrnes' book *Catholic Bishops in American Politics* (Princeton University Press, Princeton, New Jersey, 1991).

Chapter 10 — Additional Catholic Patriots

Sources used for this chapter included Albert J. Nevins' *Our American Catholic Heritage* (Our Sunday Visitor, Huntington, Indiana, 1972), Theodore Roemer's *The Catholic Church in the United States* (B. Herder Book Co., St. Louis, 1950), Patrick H. Ahern's *The Life of John J. Keane* (Bruce Publishing Co., Milwaukee, 1955), Benjamin J. Blied's *Catholics and the Civil War* (Bruce Publishing Co., Milwaukee, 1945),

Roy J. Honeywell's *Chaplains of the United States Army*, John L. Spalding's *Life of the Most Rev. M.J. Spalding*, John H. Lamott's *History of the Archdiocese of Cincinnati*, Fr. Francis P. Duffy's *Father Duffy's Story*, Raymond Kerrison's *Bishop Walsh of Maryknoll*, Thomas C. Reeves' *America's Bishop* (Encounter Books, San Francisco, 2002), and Robert I. Gannon's *The Cardinal Spellman Story*.

Our Sunday Visitor ...
Your Source for Discovering the Riches of the Catholic Faith

Our Sunday Visitor has an extensive line of materials for young children, teens, and adults. Our books, Bibles, pamphlets, CD-ROMs, audios, and videos are available in bookstores worldwide.

To receive a FREE full-line catalog or for more information, call **Our Sunday Visitor** at **1-800-348-2440, ext. 3**. Or write **Our Sunday Visitor** / 200 Noll Plaza / Huntington, IN 46750.

Please send me ____ A catalog
Please send me materials on:
____ Apologetics and catechetics
____ Prayer books
____ The family
____ Reference works
____ Heritage and the saints
____ The parish

Name _____
Address _____ Apt._____
City _____ State _____ Zip_____
Telephone ( ) _____
                                                          A49BBBBP

Please send a friend ____ A catalog
Please send a friend materials on:
____ Apologetics and catechetics
____ Prayer books
____ The family
____ Reference works
____ Heritage and the saints
____ The parish

Name _____
Address _____ Apt._____
City _____ State _____ Zip_____
Telephone ( ) _____
                                                          A49BBBBP

OurSundayVisitor

200 Noll Plaza, Huntington, IN 46750
Toll free: **1-800-348-2440**
Website: www.osv.com